100 WINEMAKING PROBLEMS ANSWERED

by Cedric Austin

© The Amateur Winemaker Ltd. 1975

Published by The Amateur Winemaker Ltd.
South Street, Andover

1st Impression
2nd Impression, December 1976
3rd Impression, October 1977
4th Impression, October 1978
5th Impression, October 1979
6th Impression, September 1981

SBN 0 900841 41 9

Printed in Great Britain by
Standard Press (Andover) Ltd., South Street, Andover, Hants.
Tel. (0264) 2413

OTHER BOOKS ON WINE
BY THE SAME AUTHOR

The Science of Wine *U.L.P.*
Whys and Wherefores of Winemaking *A.W.*
The Good Wines of Europe *A.W.*

We argued the thing at breakfast,
We argued the thing at tea,
And the more we argued the question,
The more we didn't agree.

William Carleton

SUBJECTS COVERED

I. PREPARATIONS
1. Invert Sugar
2. Just a Gimmick
3. Chlorine in Water
4. Wine Bufferage
5. Value of Extra Yeast
6. The Air Lock
7. Fluoridation
8. Palate *v.* Titration
9. Hard Water
10. A Mouldy Must
11. Cloudy Syrup
12. Cereals and Alcohol
13. C.G.J. for Sweetening
14. Vitamins
15. Liquid Paraffin
16. Sweet and Low
17. Wine Yeasts
18. Choose Your Sulphite
19. Spontaneous Fermentation
20. Grape Concentrate
21. Friend or Foe?
22. Cane or Beet
23. A Non-Starter
24. Testing for Tannin
25. Potential Alcohol
26. The Tardy Orange
27. Which Acid?
28. Grapes and Flowers
29. Better Never than Late
30. Rhubarb! Rhubarb!
31. Behind My Back
32. More Colour Wanted

II. RESULTS
33. Cloudy Blends
34. Excess Acid
35. Ullage Trouble

36. Age and Alcohol
37. Pasteurisation
38. Lack of Bouquet
39. Glucose Haze
40. Store Life
41. Sweet and Low
42. Unsettled
43. A Bit Thick
44. Browned Off
45. Unwanted Sherry
46. Potato Hangover
47. Natural Clearing
48. Dreaded Mouse
49. Now You See It
50. Persistent Fog
51. The Long Wait
52. The Case for not Racking
53. Milk Sugar
54. Ready for the Bottle
55. Excess Sulphite
56. Sugar Stickers
57. Too Much Tannin
58. Artificial Sweeteners
59. Maderised Wine
60. Flowers of Wine
61. Helping a Malo-Lactic
62. For Better or Worse
63. Curing Oxidation
64. Floating Yeast
65. Maturing in Cask
66. A Use for Everything
67. Acetic Wine
68. A Curious Haze
69. Alcohol Checks
70. Stuck Again
71. Very Dry Wines
72. Sugar Testing
73. Serious Doubts
74. Glycerine
75. Late Clouding

III. GENERAL
76. Fusel Oil
77. Titration Query
78. Sweet or Dessert
79. Fixed or Variable
80. Japanese Saké
81. Campden Tablets
82. Hydrometer Tables
83. Wine Yeast Flavours
84. Gypsum Addition
85. Fortifying Desserts
86. A Stabilizer
87. Space Age
88. Copying Commercials
89. Cleaning Casks
90. Plastic Advice
91. Judge Bashing
92. The Little Extra
93. Ever Onward
94. Commercial Gimmicks
95. Hard Water
96. Helpful Clubs
97. Judges Quizzed
98. Proof Spirit
99. The French Way
100. The Last Word

PREFACE

This book answers a wide selection of the problems and uncertainties encountered by winemakers in the course of their hobby.

For the last five years I have kept notes of all questions I have personally heard asked about winemaking. They have occurred at quiz panels, at judges-at-the-bar sessions, at club meetings, in letters and even in the street. Like Pepys, I have jotted them down in the evening before they have escaped my memory—"and so to bed".

My purpose at the time was to discover where the main problems lay, to assess the general difficulties, and then by various means assist the winemaker to make better wine. Only recently did it occur to me that a more direct way of doing this was to publish a selection of the questions themselves, together with answers: hence *100 Wine Making Problems Answered*.

I have rearranged the questions in my own words. This has lost their personal quality, but it certainly gets to the point with the minimum of fuss, which is what the reader wants. Of course, experts may differ from some of my opinions—winemaking would be dull if everyone thought on identical lines—but I hope the answers will be found sensible and reliable. They have been grouped loosely into three divisions: Preparations, Results and General.

This book has really 101 authors. If any of the 100 winemakers who asked the questions read this preface, please accept my thanks. I should not have written it without your help.

INVERT SUGAR

1. *I notice that some firms advertise "invert sugar" for winemaking. How does it differ from ordinary sugar?*

Yeast cannot begin to ferment "ordinary" sugar, which chemists call sucrose, until it has been split into the two simpler unit-sugars which compose it. These are glucose and fructose. Fortunately, yeast contains, in addition to its fermenting enzymes, an enzyme capable of breaking down the sucrose in this way prior to fermentation. This enzyme is known as invertase, and the process itself is called inversion. Therefore, ordinary sugar is quite satisfactory for a fermentation.

However, you can if you wish by-pass this preparatory action of the yeast in the must, by purchasing sugar that has already been inverted on a commercial scale. It consists of a mixture of the simple sugars, glucose and fructose, in equal quantities. Notice that if you use this, rather more is needed by weight. This is because of the water it contains.

See also Question 2.

JUST A GIMMICK?

2. *I have been told that commercial invert sugar is just an expensive sales gimmick, since the winemaker can apparently make his own quite easily. Can you tell me how to do this?*

You can certainly invert your own sucrose, and some winemakers like to do so. Such sugar is useful for any wines that may seem to have a habit of slow starting. Otherwise yeast is quite capable of doing its own inversion, a much faster process than fermentation, so that the latter is not usually held up by the process. In addition, sucrose in an acid solution tends to split up on its own account.

To invert your sugar, put 8 lb. of sugar in 2 pints of water with ½ teaspoon of citric or tartaric acid. Bring to the boil, stirring for half an hour. Add water, rather more than two pints, to make up to a gallon. There is 1 lb. of invert sugar in each pint.

But if you purchase invert sugar, you are not being taken for a ride. This should have been manufactured from raw cane sugar (check this), and therefore it contains additional flavouring properties which have not been "purified" out.

Further, it contains a number of sugars or sugar sources, such as araban and xylan, which being pentose sugars are not fermentable by wine yeast. These, with reversion products (such as difructopyranose anhydride and related fructosans) contribute considerably to the body of the wine. Such substances may be present to the extent of 6%.

Frankly, you must try invert sugar for yourself, and only then can you pronounce upon its value for winemaking. But you are not necessarily being gulled by the manufacturers, as some winemakers insist, for it is not the same thing as the invert sugar you make yourself from ordinary sugar.

See also Question 1.

CHLORINE IN WATER

3. *The chlorine content of our water is so high at times that it can be smelt. I feel that it may affect our wine made with it. What can be done about it?*

It is dispersed by boiling, and if you feel that it is heavy for your district, it would be advisable to do so. It is quite true that in some parts of the country one can smell it from a tumbler. Remember to aerate your boiled water to replace the oxygen also removed, or you may have a sluggish start to the fermentation.

On the other hand, the sulphite you add to your must removes it by chemical action, and you might double the amount usually added in order to do this, because naturally some of the sulphite will be tied up in the process.

See also Question 7.

WINE BUFFERAGE

4. *I have been doing acid titration tests of some commercial wines, and am surprised to find them higher than I expected. They are certainly higher than the level that I find acceptable for my own wines. Why is this?*

This is true. 3·5 p.p.t. is an average figure for home-made wine, and you may find a Saint Emilion claret with 4·45 p.p.t. a Chianti with 4·2 p.p.t., a Rheingau Hock with 5·5 p.p.t., although of course they vary individually with the district and vintage.

The reason is that commercial wines consist of pure juice,

whereas it is normal for us to use water with the juice of the ingredients. As a result of this, commercial wines have more "bufferage" or, if you like, more "body". This means that the *intensity* of the acid, measured in terms of pH, is held in check by the bufferage and does not increase with added *amounts* of acid. As a consequence, commercial wine will take more acid without an unpleasant effect on the palate, with its added advantage of more ester formation.

If you want to add acid nearer to the commercial level, raise the bufferage of your wine by adding grape concentrate or even the juice from simmered bananas. In moderation, the original flavour should not be radically affected.

See also Questions 13 and 20.

VALUE OF EXTRA YEAST
5. *Can I get more alcohol in my wine by adding a larger amount of yeast at the start?*

No, you will not, and this addition of extra quantities of yeast is not recommended. You are wasting money, and you will neither get more alcohol nor improve your fermentation. The correct amount of strongly fermenting yeast in the starter bottle added to the must in a pail with access to air, allows ample amount of yeast to form before transferring the must to your fermentation jar with air-lock, where it can then get on with its job of converting sugar to alcohol. What is more, this supply of yeast will then have been reproduced in the same must which it is going to ferment, so that it is thoroughly acclimatised to its environment. You cannot improve on this situation.

See also Question 6 and 52.

THE AIR LOCK
6. *It seems to me to be too late to protect wine by adding an air-lock after the must has spent a day or two in an open pail. Why not clap on an air-lock right from the start and be safe?*

Yeast needs the presence of air for the oxygen it contains, in order to multiply effectively. When there is free access to air, yeast growth is at its maximum, but alcohol production is at its minimum. It is when air is excluded that the position is reversed; yeast growth is very slow, but yields of alcohol are high.

Consequently we conduct our initial fermentation in the presence of air, usually in a plastic pail. The must is protected by being sulphited, by the presence of acid and by a clean cloth over the pail. The supply of yeast now builds up from the minute amount added from the starter bottle until sufficient is reproduced, by the cells budding, to carry out the fermentation.

Once in the fermentation jar with air excluded by the air-lock, the real conversion of sugar to alcohol starts, and the level of yeast growth remains about constant, the amount reproduced being about equal to the amount that dies.

See also Questions 5 and 52.

FLUORIDATION

7. *Do you think that fluoridation can be responsible for a crop of sticking wines I have had lately?*

No, look elsewhere for your trouble. Fluorine does inhibit yeast, but not in the quantities to be found in your water supply. The usual amount of sodium fluoride approved for addition to a water supply is 1 p.p.m. The maximum limits set for drinking water are 2·4 p.p.m. for cool climates and 1·4 p.p.m. for warm climates, where of course more water is drunk. These proportions will not affect your fermentation unless it was a very weak one from the start for other reasons.

See also Question 3.

PALATE *V.* TITRATION

9. *Don't you think in the way instruments can be misleading that the palate is better than a titration test for acid content?*

Yes, if your palate is trained and experienced. The palate is of course what matters in judging a mature wine, and if there is disagreement between the effect on a discerning palate and a scientific measurement, then the judgment must be given to the palate, for wine is made to be drunk, not chemically analysed.

But notice that this refers to the *finished* wine. It is another matter when balancing the must, for the effect of the sugar content among other things, makes it difficult for the palate to reach a decision. It is at this early stage in particular that a titration test comes into its own and proves so valuable to the earnest winemaker.

HARD WATER

9. *I have moved to a very hard water district, and find that my wines, especially the flower wines, are turning out much smoother. They seem to have improved in this way too regularly for it to be a coincidence. Is this possible?*

Yes. In districts where water is only of medium hardness, the magnesium and calcium salts of "temporary hardness" predominate in the supply. These are bicarbonates, which precipitate out when the water is boiled, furring up the kettles and saucepans. You are now using water containing instead a preponderance of sulphates, salts known as of "permanent hardness".

Beer makers know how carbonates can ruin delicate pale ales by the harsh and unpalatable hop extract resulting from the use of water containing them. And most of us know too the old pull-up cafe trick of using bicarbonate of soda in the tea urn, giving a rough cup of tea while reducing the amount of tea leaves needed.

I am inclined to think that bicarbonates in water used for wine can likewise result in a harsh wine. Anyone who suspects these in his water supply from the heavy furring of kettles, might experiment with boiled water in winemaking, remembering to replace the oxygen boiled out by various means of agitation before using.

See also Question 95.

A MOULDY MUST

10. *I balanced my must carefully, added two Campden tablets, and then set it aside with a clean cloth over it while I went on to get the yeast starter going. When I looked again at the must to add the starter, which had proved troublesome, it was covered with a greeny-white film. What had I missed?*

You hadn't missed anything; your trouble is the old one with beginners of a time-lag between the preparation of the must and the innoculation of it with the yeast starter.

It is essential to remember that sulphur-dioxide, the sterilising ingredient of Campden tablets, is a temporary and not a permanent barrier against infection. When added to the must, it moves to a peak after about twenty-four hours, dealing a knock-out blow at resident wild yeasts and bacteria in the must, which takes the full shock of it. Then as its power starts to wane, the activated wine yeast, with a built-in resistance to sulphite, is added, and a strong fermentation should quickly develop to swamp late recovery by unwanted yeasts and moulds.

So often beginners have a spot of bother at first with yeast starter bottles, with the result that the must is left for several days or even longer, and either the moulds recover or fresh spores enter the must, as the activity of the free sulphur-dioxide falls back. This is the origin of the film on your must.

The answer is always to get your yeast started *before* you prepare the must. Then your priorities are right, and this dangerous time-lag will not occur in the event of a reluctance to start on the part of the yeast.

See also Question 31.

CLOUDY SYRUP

11. *I prepare sugar syrup in advance, and occasionally lately it has gone cloudy with what looks like strands of silk in it. Is it all right to use?*

This could be a wild yeast infection. for there are species that can attack a sugar solution, but it is far more likely to have been contaminated by a water mould.

The way to prevent this occurring is to keep your syrup in smaller containers, so that once opened the whole quanity is used and, secondly, to fill these while the syrup is still hot. This latter action will avoid the infection getting into the syrup between the period of cooling and bottling, while it stands about in an open pan.

In addition, and particularly in your case, sterilise the containers between batches with metabisulphite or other sterilising solutions.

CEREALS AND ALCOHOL

12. *Can one increase the alcohol content of wine by the addition of a cereal such as rice or maize?*

No, not the ethyl alcohol content. There is an idea about that this is so, probably because the cereal flavour resulted in old recipes having such names as Potato Whisky, but it is incorrect.

The reason is that wine yeast cells do not ferment starch (although there exists a yeast found in flour called *Endomycopsis* that can), because the enzymes capable of breaking down starch into fermentable sugars remain inside the cell, and the starch molecule is too large to penetrate the cell membrane. Only when the starch molecule is broken down into glucose, as during the malting of barley for beer production, can the yeast cell start fermenting it. These cereal ingredients therefore, can only give flavour and some extra body to the must containing them, not alcohol.

There is always the possibility, however, that autolysis (or break up) of yeast cells which have completed their life cycle may take place in the must, and intracellular enzymes be released, which can then attack the starch present to give glucose. Thus a sugar increase *could* take place to give extra alcohol, but the amount would probably be very slight.

With cereals and potatoes, it should be pointed out that larger than usual amounts of higher alcohols, known collectively as Fusel Oil, may be produced. These take their origin not from sugar but from the amino acids present in the ingredients, and it could be that their presence has boosted the idea that wines made from such ingredients carry a punch. They can certainly carry a headache if over-indulged in.

See also Questions 46, 76 and 80.

C.G.J. FOR SWEETENING

13. *Several members of our Club are using concentrated grape juice to sweeten up their dry wines for competition purposes, claiming that its natural sugar content is an advantage; together with increased body, vinosity and bouquet. But is this fair?*

I see no reason why this is not fair, always provided that competition regulations do not forbid anything other than the named ingredient. Very many winemakers use C.G.J. as an additive to their musts and to their wines, just as the old timers used raisins.

Bear in mind, however, that your are not just adding grape

sugar. C.G.J. contains tannin and acid, as well as sulphite, so that the balance may be disturbed where this is added to a *completed* wine, an important point to consider when entering a competition. The careful winemaker either anticipates this later addition by reducing tannin and acid in the original must, or keeps the fiinshed wine after adding the grape concentrate until smoothing out is completed. In the latter case refermentation may start up again for a time if the weather is warm.

See also Questions 4 and 20.

VITAMINS
14. *I have noticed in some modern recipes that a Vitamin-B tablet is included. This never occurred in old books of recipes, why is it included now? Is it really necessary?*

It was not included in recipes by our grandmothers because they did not know about such things. Without their being aware of it, the vitamins got into the must from the ingredients used, especially the raisins beloved of old recipe compilers. Then too there was the slice of floating toast!

It is not necessary to include a vitamin-B tablet if this vitamin is present in the ingredients, but since one cannot always be certain of this it is a useful precaution to add a 3 mg. tablet of B1, Aneurine or Thiamine Hydrochloride.

A must may contain both sugar and nitrogen in solution, the two main needs of yeast, and have a poor fermentation because of a deficiency in certain minerals and vitamins. The most important minerals and minerals salts needed in trace amounts, are the metals potassium and magnesium and the salts sulphates and phosphates. The vitamins needed belong to the B-group, particularly B1. Without these substances the enzyme systems cannot function properly, and so a delayed fermentation ensues.

Your recipe therefore follows modern practice in ensuring that the yeast has all its requirements for a strong fermentation.

LIQUID PARAFFIN
15. *My wife called my attention to the fact that liquid paraffin was given on the pack of raisins as an ingredient. What is*

the purpose of this and is it detrimental to a fermentation when these are used as ingredients in wine?

This seems to be quite a common practice nowadays, the idea being to "lubricate" the raisins or sultanas packed together so that they do not stick. It is harmless enough in the sense that it is not toxic, having once been popular as a laxative but it is undesirable in a must for it can form an oily seal over the surface of the must, thus excluding its contact with air.

To remove the oil, soak the raisins for an hour in warm water, separating them with the fingers so that the oil can float to the surface. Then remove this from the top of the water with blotting paper. Do not take out the ingredients until this has been done, or it will be picked up by them again.

SWEET AND LOW

16. *Is it possible successfully to produce a sweet wine of limited alcohol content, the sweetness being of residual sugar after fermentation has ceased?*

It is not easy to see why anyone should want a combination of sweetness with low alcohol, but perhaps the answer is the old one of its being a challenge. A sweet wine really needs plenty of alcohol to carry the sugar.

The fact is that it is difficult suddenly to stop a fermentation when it is in full swing, unless one poisons the yeast with massive doses of sulphite and so spoils the wine, or raises the alcohol content by adding spirit, as is done commercially with port, so that the yeast is inhibited from working by its presence.

However, if you *must* halt a wine with residual alcohol and sugar to the level that you require, try any of these methods.

1. Rack somewhat prior to the stage where you want the fermentation to stop. Fermentation will start again slowly, and as soon as there is a thin layer of yeast at the bottom, rack again. This racking cuts back on the yeast population of the must, and it will help if when balancing the must you go easy with yeast nutrient. Finish by sulphiting at 50 p.p.m.

2. Rack twice as above, and then add the maximum of sorbic acid recommended, about 1 gm. in a gallon, available as Sorbistat K. This is a powerful yeast and mould inhibitor.

3. Choose a Moselle yeast, which will not ferment beyond about 9% alcohol content, and so will cease at this stage leaving residual unfermented sugar in the wine. Again, restrict nutrient salts at the time of balancing, and sulphite lightly at the close of the fermentation.

WINE YEASTS

17. *I am thinking of changing to "wine yeasts". I can understand the general benefits that these bring to winemakers but is there any point in bothering about district names? I can't believe that a Burgundy yeast will make me a Burgundy wine.*

It won't—on its own account. These wine yeasts need matching with suitable musts if the utmost benefit is to be derived from them.

The highly individual character of commercial wines is due to at least four basic factors: the variety of vine used; the soil and position where the vine is grown; the climate and topography of the district; the viticulture and the vinification employed. Over the centuries local strains of yeasts have adapted themselves to these environmental factors, so that they match up perfectly with the must from the pressed grapes to provide outstanding and distinctive wines.

Obviously then you cannot take a wine yeast from a red Burgundy district, drop it into a parsnip must, and expect to get a Beaujolais wine! If this is your aim, you have to support the yeast by matching up your must as close as possible to the French original, and it is certainly astonishing what can be done in this respect.

More usually, winemakers rest content in choosing a wine yeast to correspond fairly loosely with the type of wine they are making; a German Hock yeast for a light-white must low in sugar content; a Sauternes yeast for a heavy sweet white must—and so on. In this way, the yeast finds itself in similar surroundings to those in which it was bred, and time and energy is not spent in having to acclimatise itself to a strange, and perhaps unsuitable, environment.

See also Question 82.

CHOOSE YOUR SULPHITE

18. *I understand that there are two types of metabisulphite. What is the difference and which is the best for a stock solution?*

Potassium Metabisulphite is the more soluble of the two—although users of Campden tablets might argue about this! Sodium Metabisulphite is not only a little cheaper, but it contains 119 parts of sulphur dioxide, the active ingredient, to 104 parts in the case of the Potassium form.

The Sodium form is recommended for your stock solution, unless of course you are on a diet for blood pressure and must avoid this at all costs. Two ounces made up to a pint give a 10% solution, providing about 5% sulphur dioxide in solution. 10 mls. of this is used for a gallon, roughly equivalent to 2 Campden tablets. Remember to keep your stock solution tightly stoppered and in a cool place.

See also Question 81.

SPONTANEOUS FERMENTATION

19. *A lecturer recently mentioned in passing that our grandmothers made wine without adding any yeast. I wasn't able to question him, but wonder whether he had his facts right.*

This is one of those statements that should be qualified, although perhaps the speaker assumed that the audience followed what he really meant. He must have been aware that no yeast=no fermentation.

He was referring to an old, and one hopes now extinct, habit of preparing a must and then leaving it without adding any yeast. As a result, since it is open to the air and unsulphited, all the bacteria, wild yeasts and mould spores around at the time make a dive for the prepared banquet. Among the yeasts arriving will certainly be representatives of the "apiculates", which are common on fruit and may therefore already be in the must with the ingredients. These start fermenting very rapidly, but produce a small amount of alcohol and a high amount of acid. They tend to leave behind a cider-like wine, probably with considerable residual sugar and odd side-flavours.

This is known as spontaneous fermentation, and of course although no yeast has been introduced, it is the result of wild yeasts that have "added" themselves. The wine made in such a way is usually putrid, although from time to time, by sheer chance and rule of thumb, a drinkable wine results.

GRAPE CONCENTRATE

20. *What are your views on the use of concentrated grape juice, both as a straight wine and as an additive to other ingredients?*

I have judged many C.G.J. classes in shows, and recently had the occasion to taste and comment on over 100 wines made by wine clubs all over the country from various grape concentrates.

The conclusions on the whole are not very favourable: while some were really close to commercial wines, some were undrinkable, and the majority just dull. Your own wine made from C.G.J. could come in any of these three divisions, and I cannot forecast the result. Commercial methods of concentration vary, some employing crude evaporation but others modern vacuum-pan methods, and winemakers themselves have a wide range of ability. A general impression is that useful general-purpose plonk can be made from grape concentrate, with the minimum of fuss and bother.

Beginners are naturally attracted by the simplicity of making such wines, but it seems that the general use of concentrated grape juice by experienced winemakers is as an *additive* to wines using some other ingredients as their base.

With wines made from ingredients low in essentials for a good fermentation, its use is indispensible for producing a balanced wine. The addition of C.G.J. of the appropriate colour from a cupful to a pint in a gallon, results in increased bouquet, body and, above all, vinosity. You get a wine, not a nice smelling mixture of alcohol and water.

Even with fruits, C.G.J. can be of real advantage if the bufferage (or thickness if you like) is low. In such cases, although the *amount* of acid may be correct as indicated by a titration test, the pH or *intensity* of the acid is not held in check by the bufferage of the must, and the resulting wine may be sharp and rough on the palate. This is often the case where less than 4 lb. of fruit is used.

Minimal ingredients, such as elderberry or Ribena, need at least 1 pint of grape concentrate per gallon of must. Then your pH will be within reasonable limits and you can add the normal amount of acid, thus keeping your must safe against bacteria and achieving a wine that is smoother and more vinous.

See also Questions 4 and 13.

FRIEND OR FOE?
21. *The bacteria that produce the helpful malo-lactic fermentation are* Lactobacilli, *but so, I have read, are other species of bacteria which can cause all sorts of trouble. How can one separate these different species, admitting one sort and keeping out the other?*

A really good question! As you say, all sorts of troubles can arise from the *Lactobacilli* range, including cheesy, bitter and mousy flavours. (One school of thought attributes the notorious "mousiness" to *Bacterium gayoni* and *B. intermedium*.) In addition, they can cause turbidity in wine, which includes a shimmering kind of ropiness and a clear slime at the bottom of the jar.

Fortunately, the different species of *Lactobacilli*, and there are many of them, vary in their acid tolerance over quite a wide range, and this affords a means of control. The naughty ones are generally sensitive to an acidic medium, being checked by a pH of 4·5. Our malo-lactic friends are more tolerant, and therefore we have a means at our disposal of separating them, the adjustment of the acid content of the must being the method. Keep up your acidity to recommended levels and you should have no trouble from lactobacillic causes, while at the same time not excluding a later malo-lactic fermentation if conditions are suitable.

All species are similar in being susceptible to sulphur dioxide, so if you do not want any of the genus at all, sulphite your must well and play safe.

See also Questions 61 and 62.

CANE OR BEET

22. *Does it make any difference to wine whether the sugar used in the must derives from sugar cane or sugar beet?*

The text-book answer to this is—No. Any scientist will tell you that chemically these two forms of sucrose are identical, the molecule of each substance being composed of identical atoms, identically arranged. Even so, some less conservative members of that superior ilk, if their arms are twisted, will admit that substances may well contain ingredients apart from those isolated and analysed, which can impart subtle nuances of bouquet and flavour to wine.

Certainly champagne manufacturers round Rheims and Epernay have told me that they always use cane sugar for their *dosage* on the grounds that beet sugar conveys an "earthy" flavour to this very delicate wine. One could dismiss this as tradition, or one could take a hint from them.

It is difficult to overcome inborn feelings that cane is "natural" and that beet is a "substitute", even when these go against logic and scientific fact. I must confess that when I notice a stock of sugar marked "cane" in our local supermarket, I stock up my wine cupboards with it and have a satisfactory sense of one-upmanship.

A NON-STARTER

23. *My must has been prepared according to the recipe, but it will not start to ferment. What have I done wrong?*

This question just had to turn up, but without some acquaintance with you or your wine making methods, it is impossible to diagnose exactly and tell you what you have done wrong. A non-starter, as distinct from a "stuck" wine, usually calls for a methodical run-through of all the main aspects of assembling the must, and therefore the best way to help you is to list these for you to follow.

1. Acid: have you brought this up to the required level? If you have any doubts at all, add half a level teaspoon of citric acid; it will do no harm.

2. Sugar: is your gravity over 100? Excessive sweetness, a characteristic both of old recipes and beginners, can dry out yeast cells by a process called osmosis so that they are inactive. Test by taking ½ pint of must, adding ¼ pint of

water, and fermenting in a bottle stoppered with cotton wool. The reverse, absence of sugar, is unlikely, although it has been known with absolute beginners.

3. Nutrient: have you added the nutrient salts to provide essential nitrogen? With some ingredients, such as flowers, these are very necessary.

4. Temperature: is your fermenting pail in a warm place, around 70°–75°F? Some wine yeasts accustomed to a warm climate demand this. On the other hand, could you have destroyed them by adding them to an over-hot must?

5. Oxygen: yeast cells must multiply at the start of a fermentation until they reach a figure where they stay more or less constant. For this reproductive period, air is necessary and open-pail fermentation for at least 24 hours is advisable, before transferring to the demi-john with air-lock. If you started directly with a jar, put into a pail, stir and cover with a clean cloth.

6. Sulphite: presumably you sulphited the must. Have you exceeded the recommended 100 p.p.t.? Have you waited 12–24 hours before adding your yeast, sometimes an old wine yeast gets a set-back when added too early.

7. Yeast: if you used a wine yeast, was it fermenting vigorously when added to the bulk of the must? Try again with a strong granulated yeast of the type that is sprinkled on the surface.

See also Question 70.

TESTING FOR TANNIN

24. *Can I do a titration test for tannin as accurately as I do for acid? Is the correct level of this as important as the right amount of acid?*

As an amateur you cannot. The test involves the use of indigo solution with N/50 potassium permanganate, but the main problem is the pre-distillation, so that it is really out of the question on practical grounds.

It therefore remains for the palate to decide whether there is sufficient present or not. It is easy enough to add it, the tannin solution being the better form, and it can also be taken out by you if excessive, although avoid this if possible as it is something of a bother.

On the whole there seems to be too little in amateur red wines, with certain notable exceptions, and it would help if winemakers tasted their products against a commercial wine of the type they are aiming for, in order to get an idea of the amount that should be present.

Flavour apart, there are other reasons just as with the acid, why the level should be carefully considered. A wine without tannin is unlikely to clear well on its own, its presence being essential for the flocculation of protein colloidal particles, and also the keeping properties of tannin are called for where a wine is put down to mature over a period of time.

See also Question 57.

POTENTIAL ALCOHOL

25. *My new hydrometer has another reading besides that of gravity, named "potential alcohol". What is the purpose of this?*

As you no doubt know, the method of estimating the amount of alcohol in finished wine is to subtract the final gravity, after the fermentation has ceased, from the original gravity at the start, and refer to tables. This gives quite a useful idea of the alcoholic situation.

More useful than this, is to be able to *forecast in advance* the level of alcohol content, so that one can produce a particular type of wine. As this depends largely on the amount of sugar present, the initial gravity reading can be used on which to base the forecast. Formerly it meant referring to tables, but most modern hydrometers now include such a potential alcohol scale on their stem. Remember, of course, that it holds true only if all your sugar is fermented out to dryness.

See also Questions 69, 78 and 82.

THE TARDY ORANGE

26. *I used a well-known recipe using oranges and their skins, but after 36 hours I cannot see a sign of fermentation. I have not made orange wine before, so is this type of wine difficult to ferment?*

It can be so, where the skins are used and they are particularly oily. What happens is that the oil is sufficient to form a thin skin over the surface, so that insufficient atmospheric oxygen is available for the yeast to reproduce well, and the resultant fermentation hangs fire.

One does not want to dispense with the skins which contain much flavour, provided the pith is removed, so try baking these first in the oven. In their dried state, the flavour is still there but the oil does not seem to cause the same bother. Also remember to aerate the must vigorously and often, pouring it from one pail to another, until your fermentation is going well.

WHICH ACID?
27. *Some recipes use citric acid, others tartaric, and I have seen malic acid included. What is to be said for and against each of these?*

These three acids are the normal organic acids found in the vegetable kingdom, and therefore the three we use as additives in our must when it is deficient in acid, as is often the case after dilution with water. Here briefly are the advantages and drawbacks of each.

Citric Acid: this is still the most popular general purpose acid, and the modern equivalent of "the juice of lemons" in old recipes. Its flavour is generally satisfactory for our purpose, clean and sharp without being too rough, and it provides an acidic medium that the yeast enjoys to provide a healthy fermentation. At the same time, bacterial visitors are discouraged by it more than by any other. Its weakness is that it is liable by reaction to bring diacetyl and also acetic acid into the must, although early sulphiting discourages this. Further, and very important, it has not the property possessed by the other two acids of increasing bouquet during maturity.

Tartaric Acid: this is a typical grape acid, and for that reason often preferred by its supporters, who say they do not want a "lemon acid" in their wine. (In fact, citric occurs in black currants and pineapples and other fruits than citrus). Its main value is its ester-forming qualities, which confer good bouquet and flavour to the wine. Against its use is its formation of potassium bi-tartrate in the wine, which being poorly soluble may bring hazes, although these precipitate out if chilled, giving the crystals known as "argol".

Malic Acid: another grape acid, although common enough in apples and much soft fruit. It is the best of the three for producing esters, a strong supporting claim. Its flavour, however, is rough, for malic is an "acid" acid, and where its presence is too evident can make a wine harsh. In addition, it can be attacked by bacteria called *Lactobacilli*, to produce a late second fermentation that causes corks to blow. At the same time, this nuisance is balanced by the fact that much malic is converted into the softer lactic acid, so largely removing the drawback just mentioned.

See also Question 38.

GRAPES AND FLOWERS

28. *When speaking to a judge of the flower class at a "Judges-at-the-bar" session, I was told that my wine was watery, and advised to add grape concentrate. I think this is cheating; what are your views?*

Show schedules tend more and more to state clearly what is expected in a certain class of wine, and what can and cannot be included in its making. This is a desirable state of affairs, for it helps judges as well as competitors to know where they are.

If your flower-class schedule does not forbid the addition of grape concentrate, then you are putting yourself at a disadvantage by not including it. Flowers are insufficient in themselves to make a vinous wine, a fact that our grandmothers knew when they specified raisins in the recipe.

The simple fact is that you cannot make good wine out of a smell, and colour apart flowers bring precious little else to the must.

BETTER NEVER THAN LATE

29. *I forgot to sulphite my must until about 48 hours after adding the yeast. It was fermenting strongly at the time. The fermentation slowed down almost at once, but then picked up again and continued to dryness. The resulting wine was a horrible smell and taste. Was I too late in sulphiting?*

Yes, but not, as you probably think, because the must has become infected owing to your oversight in neglecting to sulphite it at the beginning. The horrible smell inclines me to think that you would have done better to leave sulphiting alone, having forgotten it so far, until the first racking.

Your must would, at the stage you mention, have had the advantage of a layer of carbon-dioxide gas over it, as well as some alcohol building up in it, both safeguards against infection. A good acid content would also have been a protection.

When you added your meta-bisulphite, the strongly fermenting wine yeast endeavoured to reduce it, which is its method of avoiding its inhibiting power, and it was successful. The resultant chemical left in the must from this reaction is hydrogen sulphide, with its notorious smell of rotten eggs.

Now that your fermentation is over, you may, strange as it seems, be able to cure it by adding two more sulphite tablets or equivalent stock solution. These break up the hydrogen sulphide and precipitate sulphur that should be carried to the bottom as the wine clears.

RHUBARB! RHUBARB!

30. *When should I pull rhubarb to make wine? Everyone I ask wants to avoid the oxalic acid it contains, but there are two schools of thought about the time of pulling. Some say early, others late. Must the wine always be so thin?*

The main acid of rhubarb is malic, usually in the form of its potassium salt, and it ranges from $1 \cdot 0 – 1 \cdot 7 \%$. In addition, it contains oxalic acid, not a desirable acid in wine at all, in trace quantities in the form of oxalates. Most of this is in the leaves, and there have been cases of poisoning where these have been cooked and eaten as a spinach substitute.

The best time to pull the sticks is when young. Acid content may then be low enough to avoid neutralising it out and then replacing it. The juice can be extracted by mechanical means—even an old mangle, if such a thing still exists—or by cold water pulp fermentation, adding grape concentrate and bananas to give body and vinosity. Too often this wine is flat and dull, as you say, and can contain unpleasant odours where excess chalk has been used to counteract acidity. If bufferage is introduced in this way from other ingredients, the pH can be forgotten, and a very pleasant wine result.

BEHIND MY BACK
31. *I prepared my must and then tackled the job of starting off the yeast. This was the first time I had used a wine yeast; previously I had used the type of yeast that is sprinkled on top of the must. To my astonishment, when I went to add the yeast, the must was already working despite my having sterilised it with Campden tablets. Why was this?*

Your method, as revealed by your first sentence, is wrong. Never prepare your must until the yeast in the starter bottle is fermenting well, and will be ready to add in 12 hours or so. Then you can think about balancing the must, and sulphite it in preparation for innoculation with yeast.

Sulphiting a must does not sterilise it indefinitely, in fact it does not truly sterilise it at all, because one cannot use metabisulphite in a must at the strength employed for sterilising apparatus. What it does is to reduce any wild yeasts, mould spores and bacteria *to an acceptable level*, and hold them there until the strong wine yeasts can build themselves up and take over.

For some reason, perhaps you were not used to handling wine yeasts, there was a time lag between the time of sulphiting and adding the yeast, that was excessive. As a result, the power of the sulphur dioxide in the must waned, and wild yeasts—always very quick to start, were able to get under way. Once one is aware of this danger, there is no need at all for it to happen a second time.

See also Question 10.

MORE COLOUR WANTED
32. *I do not seem to be getting much colour from my raspberries when using pulp fermentation. Is there anything I can do to improve this?*

There is nothing much wrong with the rosé colour from raspberries, but if you really want a deeper colour, you could add a small amount of elders and bilberries, or blend these when the wine is finished.

However, if you want to keep to raspberries only, you

should cut down on sugar to the minimum to keep the fermentation going in the pail, adding the rest once the must has been strained off the pulp. The colours of fruit are water-soluble pigments known as anthocyanins, forms of glycosides. These are leached out more easily in the absence of sugar, so you should get more into your wine this way if you are at present disappointed by its weak colour. Naturally it can never be anything approaching purple from fruit of this sort.

Do you have a friend in the trade? He might get you some oenocyanine tablets, which blenders abroad have been known to use where the colour has been below standard.

CLOUDY BLENDS

33. *Why does blending two clear wines together so often result in a cloudy mixture with deposits as it clears? Sometimes even fermentation starts up again when the two come together.*

You have to remember that your blended wine, although made up from two finished wines, is now a new wine in its own right, and it needs time to adjust itself and sort itself out. All wines, provided that they are healthy, will try to work out a balance within the limitations imposed on them by their constituents, and given time will do so, unless their original make up is quite out of line in the sense of deficiencies and excesses. The new blended wine, therefore, needs time to work itself out, and until it can do so is in a state of cloudy turmoil.

To look at it from a chemical point of view, the coming together of two different wines can start a series of reactions. For instance, if one of the wines has protein instability, particularly if made from fruit, the tannin in the other wine may be just what it needs to settle out, and consequently a cloudy haze may first ensue, with later deposits as it clears. Acetaldehyde, present to a small extent in all wines but particularly those tending to oxidation, is a very reactive compound which will react with colour pigments, called anthocyanins, to throw out an insoluble dark pigment in red wines. It will also precipitate tannic acid in solution in the form of salts called tannates. Alcohol, particularly methyl alcohol, will precipitate pectin when present.

If one wine has a trace of sugar and the other some autolysed (disintegrated) yeast cells to provide nutrient, then as likely as not a short refermentation may get under way.

Wine is a living thing, and its life does not come to an end at the close of its main fermentation. The reactions of two blended wines help us to remember this fact.

EXCESS ACID
34. *My gooseberry wine is far too acid to drink. How can I make it palatable?*

There are two main courses open to you.

The first is to try sweetening the wine, if it is dry as are so many gooseberry wines. If you feel that the alcohol content is not enough to carry this, you could blend it with a dull sweet wine that you have already. Give the two blended wines time to adjust themselves, for you will throw things out of balance for a while by bringing them together. If you have not such a wine to use in this way, try adding grape concentrate to increase the bufferage of the wine; a pint of this in a gallon can have quite a dramatic effect, although it is not likely to result in a competition wine.

The other approach is to remove the acid by chemical means. Precipitated chalk at the rate of 1 oz. to a gallon gives a reduction of 6 p.p.t., so probably ½ oz. would do the trick, although you would be advised to control the reduction by titration tests, or you may finish with an alkaline wine. Another addition to reduce acid that is gaining ground among winemakers, is potassium carbonate. It is soluble and less messy. Dissolve 9 oz. in water to make 1 pint. Then a fluid ounce of this in one gallon will reduce your acidity by 2 p.p.t., and the wine still remains clear.

ULLAGE TROUBLE
35. *When I take out a bottle of wine for show purposes, I am anxious about the quantity of air left in my demijohn. What can be done about this ullage?*

The most obvious suggestion to avoid oxidation, especially with white wines, is to transfer the remaining wine into a

½-gallon jar and two wine bottles, although there seem to be other ways of dealing with the problem. I knew a winemaker who kept sterilised glass marbles, large ones, which he slid into the jar until the level reached its former height.

An alternative is to do what the commercial boys do with bulk wine from which amounts are drawn off from time to time. Pour in a layer of oil to cover the surface of the wine. It will not mix with the wine, and you can syphon off below it, the layer sinking as the level falls. Olive oil contains something of an off-flavour, so use a vegetable oil of a more neutral kind, such as sun-flower seed.

AGE AND ALCOHOL

36. *A country friend gave me a glass of very special wine, saying that it was eight years old, and that age had made it as strong as whisky. It seemed pretty feeble to me, but is there anything in this idea?*

This is an old wives' tale that dies hard among winemakers, particularly those with no knowledge of theory. Ethyl alcohol, the basic alcohol of wine, is formed by the fermentation of sugar, and if this had continued during storage the gas formed would have set off the bottle like a bomb. Obviously, then, no more alcohol had been produced during its long period in the cellar.

This is not to disregard the fact that other alcohols in wine, notably methyl alcohol and fusel oil, are not connected with the fermentation process and have other origins, but they exist in traces only, and this co-relation of age and strength is largely nonsense. The only concession that can be made to it is where the wine has been stored in cask in dry conditions so that evaporation of the water content has been taking place from the surface of the cask. The proportion of alcohol to water might then be somewhat higher, as time passes, but in the damp conditions of this country the reverse is usually the case.

See also Question 65.

PASTEURISATION

37. *I am fed up with a batch of wine that will keep refermenting whenever the weather turns warm. Stabilisers have been added, yet still the corks blow. What do you suggest?*

Unless you intend to keep it for show purposes, the best method, although perhaps a drastic one, is to pasteurise it. This will settle the tendency to referment once and for all.

Place wooden slats on the bottom of your fruit-bottling saucepan, loosen the corks, and fill the pan with water as high as convenient. Heat the water to 140°F, and hold it there for 20 minutes, or if you have no thermometer, simmer the water for this time. Remember to sterilise your corks too in boiling water for the same period before finally corking down the wine.

Any yeast cells in the wine will now have been destroyed, and therefore no further fermentation, including malo-lactic, should take place, leaving the wine completely stable. Of course, your wine is dead in the sense that development has been permanently arrested at this point, and there is no point in retaining it for a long period. It will keep, but it will not mature.

LACK OF BOUQUET

38. *When I smell commercial wines, I am impressed by the fragrance of the bouquet. My wines have a satisfactory flavour, but I cannot seem to get this fine bouquet. It is there, but one has to search around for it. Why is this?*

This seems to be a weakness of many home made wines, and judges would probably agree that the absence of a bouquet that rises up to meet the nose when the cork is removed is not an uncommon defect in many wines.

Probably, as much as anything, this is an acid problem. Bouquet turns largely on the odiferous esters formed during maturation between alcohols and acids. Some acids lend themselves to this formation more easily and effectively than others, and of the three acids normally used in wine, the order of esterification is malic, tartaric, citric. Citric acid is a good all-round acid for winemaking purposes, but where this is the sole acid, little vinous bouquet is present in the finished wine.

You should experiment therefore in avoiding an all-citric balance in your musts. As you know, grape juices have either tartaric or malic as their main acid. Try experimenting with mixtures of all three, such as Citric+Malic+Tartaric in the proportion of 1/2/3, and then use this mixture to adjust the acid of your must in the usual way.

Interest has been taken lately in succinic acid for purposes of flavour and bouquet. This is an acid produced during fermentation, and if you are prepared to leave your wine for over a year to mature, it can help in this way. Add 2 gms or ½ teaspoon towards the close of fermentation, or after the first racking.

As a simple way out, if you do not want to be bothered by experiments with acids, add a cupful of grape concentrate to a gallon of your must. It need not affect the basic flavour, and with its tartaric and malic acid content will go some way towards your problem of bouquet.

See also Question 27.

GLUCOSE HAZE

39. *To try out the merits of glucose, I made two identical gallons of wine, one using glucose and the other ordinary grocer's sugar. The latter is clearing well, but the glucose has a haze. Can this be due to the glucose?*

Since the two gallons of wine are otherwise identical, there seems little doubt that the haze originates from the glucose. This substance, like anything else, varies in quality, and you would seem to have an inferior sort where not all of the starch has been hydrolised into glucose. As a result, you have a starch haze in your wine.

To test for this, pour a tablespoonful or so of wine into a small glass and add a few drops of iodine. Stir, and if starch is present the brown colour changes to blue. Treat your wine with Amylase, a starch-destroying enzyme used in a similar way to pectinase, and your wine will eventually be as clear as the other batch.

See also Question 68.

STORE LIFE

40. *I should like to know what is the store life of the liquid in my titration outfit. I have been told by friends that it quickly deteriorates.*

You are referring to the alkaline solution of sodium hydroxide, which you drip into your test tube to neutralise the acid in the wine being tested.

Sodium hydroxide, if left unattended or loosely stoppered, will absorb carbon dioxide from the atmosphere, and so change into sodium bicarbonate. Such a variation will affect your calculations, and this is what your friends have in mind.

What affects the solution is not so much the air above the liquid in the bottle, but the frequent opening for tests and, of course, loose stoppering.

Therefore always stopper tightly and quickly when carrying out your tests. The shelf life will then depend on the frequency with which you do tests, but a fairly safe estimate is six months if used weekly, and one month if used daily, so there is not much need to worry about on this score.

If you have bought a large amount in bulk, fill smaller bottles from this, which contain enough for one or for six months, according to the rate at which you use it. Throw away any left after this time, and use a fresh bottle.

SWEET AND LOW

41. *Why does my wine still taste sweet when the hydrometer reads 0? Is the hydrometer at fault? I have heard of the need to adjust these at times.*

Your hydrometer is doing its job excellently, so do not buy another to replace it.

A gravity reading of 0° (S.G.=1·000) would represent an absence of sugar if we were working with a simple solution of sugar and water. But in the case of wine, the sugar has largely been replaced by alcohol, and it is this that complicates matters.

Alcohol has a negative gravity below that of water, so obviously the presence of alcohol in your wine will pull the hydrometer reading down, just as the presence of sugar will push it up. Both factors must be taken into account in considering the implications of a gravity reading on a hydrometer. You are thinking only of sugar and forgetting the effect of the alcohol.

If you have a completely dry wine with an average amount of alcohol, then the hydrometer will certainly show an S.G. *below* 1·000, despite the further complication of some suspended and dissolved solids which, like sugar, will tend to raise the figure. In general, however, it is safe to say that one would expect your wine with its gravity of 0° still to contain some residual sugar, and your palate has confirmed this act.

See also Questions 71, 72 and 73.

UNSETTLED

42. *I prefer to store my wine quite dry to avoid a secondary fermentation, and then to sweeten with sugar syrup if a sweet wine is wanted. Even so, there always seems to be a batch that starts up when the weather turns warm. I am not keen on pasteurising it, because I want it to continue maturing. What do you advise?*

The general answer to this is to sulphite at racking time more heavily than you usually do, but the drawback is the sulphur smell, so reminiscent of cheap commercial plonk. Apart from these unpleasant associations, many people object to it on its own account, the sensitivity varying from person to person. There is one well-known judge who sneezes when he sniffs the merest trace, because of a prickling it causes in his nose.

Commercial stabilisers make frequent use of benzoic acid, usually in the form of sodium benzoate, well-known as a food preservative and corrosion inhibitor. This is excellent with fruit juices and fruit drinks, but not so successful with alcoholic products unless large amounts are used, although it is innocuous enough.

A more reliable additive is sorbic acid, so called because it is found in the Mountain Ash, whose Latin name is *Sorbus*. It is used in the form of potassium sorbate, its function being to inhibit the growth of yeasts and moulds. This selective fungistatic for winemakers is available as Sorbistat K, which is employed at the rate of 1 gm per gallon of wine.

At one time this was not permitted in commercial wines but in Aug. 1974 its use was made legal so any doubts about its safety have been removed. The World Health Organisation agrees to its restricted use, and commercial wines both on the Continent and in America can take advantage of it, the FDA allowing up to 1000 mgs per litre. Use 1 gm per gallon.

Finally, for the sake of completeness, one should notice the value of vitamin C, which is ascorbic acid. This will not tackle the yeast cells themselves as do benzoic and sorbic acids, but it will mop up any excess oxygen in the wine originating perhaps from careless racking. If it is this that is encouraging refermentation, then its the addition of vitamin C tablets may do the trick. Quite large amounts may be added, say five 100 mg tablets to a gallon, without any toxic effect at all.

See also Question 86.

N.B. Since writing, the use of sorbic acid has now been legalised.

A BIT THICK
43. *I have moved to a country district, and now have a number of apple trees in a small orchard. Naturally I am making large amounts of apple wine, but my first batch has formed a thick layer of gummy substance at the bottom of the jar. Friends say it must be infected, but as I have never had this trouble before with this type of wine, I wonder if it is caused by the very hard water with which I dilute the juice?*

You are probably right. Without seeing the wine, I should say that it is a pectin gel, and can recall being shown this on several occasions. It would be interesting to have an analysis of the water of your district, when you would probably find that calcium salts, calcium bicarbonate and calcium sulphate, have a high content in it. These have reacted with the pectic acid of the ingredients. Apples are very strong indeed in this, commercial extracts of pectin often being manufactured from pomace, the residual pulp from cider making.

You can approach future brewing of apple wine from two angles to remove this trouble. First, you must make full use of a pectinase to break up the pectic-acid chain into smaller units of galacturonic acid, which will not gel in this fashion, and secondly, you could boil your water, which will at least remove the calcium bicarbonate salt in the water, although it will leave the calcium sulphate still present.

As you live in an unpolluted country district, you could also try using rain water, which has not, of course, been near the soil. Presumably you prefer diluted juice, as indeed do many winemakers, but you could also try a pure juice wine since you now have your own orchard.

BROWNED OFF

44. *I am pleased with my peach wine, made from fresh fruit, with one exception—namely the colour. It has a browny tinge about it, particularly noticeable when poured into the glass. Yet it is only about six months old, and I have been most careful to avoid contact with air when racking, the one occasion I did this, so I do not think it is due to this. What can be the cause?*

What is often forgotten is that oxidation, the name given to this browning of both red and white wines, can take place during the unfermented-must stage of winemaking. It is so closely associated with careless racking after fermentation, or with ullage, (excess air) in the demijohn, or with age, that the initial possibility of oxidation can be overlooked, and this seems to be the stage when your peach wine was affected.

The fact is that fresh fruit contains enzymes in the juice that will very quickly indeed bring about this rusty discoloration, once the skin is broken and air is present on the surface of the fruit. One can see this happening easily enough by cutting an apple in two, when the cut surface darkens in a matter of seconds.

What happens is that the natural enzymes in particular, known as *polyphenol oxidase*, produce oxidation by means of atmospheric oxygen of phenolic compounds, such as the anthocyanins, that give colour to the fruit. In an apple, it is the chlorogenic acid of the apple tissue that is being oxidised, but whatever are the constituents in the reaction, the result is the browning that you have noticed.

Firms marketing canned fruit juice have to deal with this problem, and use such methods as deaeration of the juice or adding glucose oxidase and catalase to mop up any oxygen present, but we winemakers usually rely on two simple precautions. First we sulphite the must quickly, and we cannot do this too quickly with such juices as apple, which tends to brown as soon as it is pressed. Metabisulphite is an excellent anti-oxidant, and it has the ability of inhibiting the enzymes present in the juice. Secondly we follow with a titration test to see that the acid content is correct, especially where the juice has been diluted. The oxidation being discussed is encouraged by a low acid level, but retarded by an increase in acidity. Adjust this as quickly as possible.

If these safeguards are followed, and precaution is taken to avoid contact with air or at least to keep it to the minimum, remembering that atmospheric oxygen assists the reaction, then this unattractive browning should be kept at bay. If however there has been a lapse somewhere along the line, drop five 10 mg. Vitamin C tablets, after crushing them, into the must as soon as possible with the hope of repairing some of the damage. Usually this is shutting the stable door too late, but perhaps it is worth trying.

See also Question 45 and 63 and 66.

UNWANTED SHERRY

45. *My wine has a curious taste that reminds me of sherry, although not a nice sherry. I was aiming at an ordinary table wine. It is also rather browny, not very noticeable in the bottle, but round the surface of the glass when poured out. I have kept it tightly corked.*

Browning can come early in the life of a wine, in fact while it is still unfermented, but in your case I am more inclined to suspect an after-fermentation oxidation for a wine with this strong sherry or "rancio" flavour. This type of late oxidation is not the same as that which takes place before fermentation, and the two reactions should not be confused.

Somewhere in its life, the wine has been in contact with air sufficiently for it to acquire this taste and discoloration. Since you have bottled carefully, one must suspect a racking or two where the wine was allowed to drop from the bottom of the racking tube through the air, or else a period when the wine was left unattended for a time, or not lightly sulphited after racking.

What has happend is this. As sugar is changed through many steps into alcohol, a substance called acetaldehyde is formed at the last step but one. An enzyme in the yeast called *alcohol dehydrogenase* brings about the reduction of this acetaldehyde to ethyl alcohol, which of course is the last step in the series of changes. Now if oxygen is available to the finished wine, the same enzyme will "back-oxidise" some of the very alcohol it produced into acetaldehyde again. Although only a small amount is changed in this way, an excess is present, and this produced the unusual "sherry" flavour that you have in your wine.

The flavour of wine is said to be affected when acetaldehyde is more than 100 p.p.m. Sherry contains more, up to 500 p.p.m., but this is its characteristic, supported by other features, such as a higher alcohol content. It is not wanted in a table wine and is objectionable as such. Incidentally, storage of wine in small barrels for too long a period is a common cause of such trouble, especially with white wine, but presumably your wine has not matured in this way.

See also Questions 44, 63 and 66.

POTATO HANGOVER

46. *I have several times come across the idea that potato wines are dangerous. Is there anything in this?*

Potato wines were very popular once, and all old recipe books include methods of making them, probably because the ingredients were so easily available in the kitchen garden.

It is still made today by its devotees, but I find it difficult to work up much enthusiasm for its flavour, which depended in old recipes largely on the raisins added. Further, it can give a nasty headache the following morning, together with a very dry mouth, although it would have to be drunk in more than usually large quantities to prove dangerous.

Grain, beetroot and potatoes bring a high proportion of two amino acids to the must called leucine and isoleucine. The result of yeast enzyme action on these is to increase the amount of fusel oil in the wine, the collective name for types of amyl and butyl alcohols. Whilst in minute quantities these can produce flavour-conferring esters in the wine, an increase in their quantity, as with the wines made from the ingredients mentioned, can bring nasty hangovers to the drinker.

If you must make these wines, introduce plenty of ammonium nutrient salts, and you have a good chance of depressing fusel oil formation.

See also Questions 12 and 76.

NATURAL CLEARING

47. *What is necessary to ensure that wine clears well of its own accord without any artificial means?*

A well-balanced must, following a steady fermentation, should drop clear of its own accord during maturation, although for one reason or another there always seems to be the exception, in which case we have to lend a hand.

Three factors combine to produce this desirable end. The first is regular racking, the second is sulphiting, the third is the presence of tannin.

Before we consider these individually, it is worthwhile considering the general cause of haze in wine. After the coarser particles of suspended matter have gravitated to the bottom, sub-microscopically small colloidal particles of proteins, pectic substances, mucillages and gums, remain suspended in the liquid. These carry an electric charge, usually positive, although beer haze is generally caused by yeast particles with a negative charge. Obviously, since these wine particles carry the same electrical charge, they repel one another, and so will stay in constant suspension unless certain factors are present to assist clarification.

Mild sulphiting at racking times, apart from other benefits such as preventing oxidation, assists clarification by neutralising to some extent the charges carried by the particles. The tannate salts of tannin carry negative charges, so that a direct combination with the protein particles is possible, thus precipitating out. And finally this process is assisted by racking, which enables the oxidation of tannin compounds to form salts, as well as oxidising soluble pigments that drop as insoluble deposits taking particles with them.

The clarification that follows can be regarded as natural, without the artificial resort to fining, although there is always the black sheep that has to be whitened by additional means.

See also Question 50.

THE DREADED MOUSE

48. *I have an off-flavour in my wine which I am told is "mousiness". What is this, and what causes it?*

First, be sure that your off-flavour *is* what is termed mousiness. Sometimes this is confused with yeastiness or a malaise that brings a soapy flavour. True mousiness has the curious characteristic of not being apparent at the first taste. You may be admiring the quality of the wine at your first mouthful, and then suddenly it hits you, a nauseating dank and close flavour that is associated with mice and their droppings.

The second characteristic is that though the bouquet may or may not convey this flavour, a few drops rubbed into the palm of the hand brings it to the attention of the nose at once, so that it seems that air accentuates it. The third quality is that palate reaction to it varies. Sometimes, a palate excellent in all other respects hardly notices it, while another is particularly sensitive to the merest suspicion. The result is that a mousy wine can cause quite a degree of disagreement among half a dozen tasters.

What is it and what causes it? There are suggestions that it is caused by a heterofermentative species of *Lactobacilli;* or by *Bacillus butyricus*, although I think personally that the flavour of these intrusive bacteria is more of rank butter; or by unpleasant amines from amino acids, such as methylamine; or by acetamide, an ammonia derivative—and so on. Until whatever causes the odour and taste is isolated we shall not know for sure. There is even the suggestion that the term arises from the French word *moisi*, but this is the term for "mouldy", quite a different flavour. And Russian chemists have claimed that it is to be associated with a long drawn out fermentation in the absence of air.

At any rate, if you are unlucky enough to have it in your wine, go over all utensils and equipment and really sterilize them, for it can persist in a home once established, a fact that points to the presence of bacteria as a cause.

NOW YOU SEE IT
49. *Although I fill my demijohn with must at the start of the ferment, it always drops in level by the end. Why is this?*
Sugar, of which 1 lb. is 10% w/v. per gallon of must, is converted during fermentation into roughly equal parts of alcohol and carbon-dioxide. The former is retained in the liquid, but of course the latter is lost into the air. This is obvious enough, but a point often forgotten is that the inversion of sucrose, assuming that this is the sugar you are

using as is generally the case, by the enzymes of the yeast involves the withdrawal of one molecule of water from your must for each molecule of sucrose thus degraded, a fact which to some extent increases the weight of the original sugar but decreases the original volume of the water. In general, an easy way of explaining the phenomenon is to say that the volume of aqueous alcohol produced is less than the volume occupied by the sugar converted, so that the final volume of must is less than the original.

If you have an additional bottle of must fermenting, as do many winemakers, you can top up your demijohn from time to time, but really there is no fear of oxidation during the fermentation; the danger arises after the fermentation has ceased and the finished wine is left with an amount of air at the top of the jar.

PERSISTENT FOG
50. *Most of my wines clear well naturally, but always there are exceptions. Is there any common factor that can be said to give rise to these?*

Wines that refuse to clear naturally are usually lacking in tannin, and have not had the benefit of regular racking together with mild sulphiting. Even so, there remain the odd instances where the cause is something peculiar to the particular case. An example is a waxy deposit on the skins of some species of plums. I once had several gallons of this which had refused every effort to clear, and in despair I used to take it along to where demonstrations of fining and filtering were taking place, to the confusion of the demonstrator. Thus it earned its keep!

But the reason for most hazy wines that will not clear is the presence of pectin. This is the most likely common factor about which you enquire. If pectin is in the wine, as when the must has not been treated with pectinase or the ingredients have been boiled, the positive charge on the colloidal protein particles is protected and stabilised, thus becoming resistant to the attraction of particles carrying an opposite charge. It is useless, in such a case, to add fining materials, for these will only create their own individual haze in addition. The pectin must first be removed.

A simple test for pectin is to shake up a tablespoon of wine with three tablespoons of methylated spirit. Pectin, if present, is precipitated as a clotted jelly at once. The wine should then be treated with pectin-destroying enzymes, such as Pectinol or Pektolase. Assuming all else is well and the tannin content is correct, the wine should now clear; if not it should be fined with Bentonite.

See also Question 47.

THE LONG WAIT

51. *Does one really need to keep wine in store for many years before drinking it if it is to realise its top quality?*

Much emphasis is placed by wine books on the need to allow wine time to mature, and for beginners this is a necessary instruction. Winemakers who have not a great deal of experience tend to regard the end of fermentation as the completion of the winemaking process. The visible changes have ceased and nothing more is obviously taking place, so surely they conclude, little more of value can happen to the wine. Support to this attitude comes from their having insufficient stocks behind them, and so the wine would doubtless be drunk at this stage if there were not the warnings of the instruction book to allow it time to mature.

Wine is a living thing, and once the fermentation has stopped other changes, slower and less visible but no less important, continue. Excess tannin and pigments, especially of reds, are thrown out as insoluble precipitates; acids combine with alcohols to form the esters that can confer bouquet and flavour; harsher acids may change to softer ones by means of a separate fermentation; acetaldehyde, a very instable and reactive substance with its carbonal groups, combines with other substances; slight oxidation continues despite the absence of air by "redox reaction"; protein instability is cancelled by tannates, and the wine clears. The wine may seem to be asleep, but a whole number of important chemical changes and reactions continue during the maturing period.

But be wary of going to the other extreme. Unfortified wine develops to a peak. Red wines take longer than white ones to reach this level, and heavy tannin-strong wines longer still. This peak may be held for a time, but then inevitably they commence to decline, to come down the slope again. So rack and taste regularly, and develop cellarcraft. When your wines are at their best, drink and enjoy them, and do not slip into the delusion that the improvement will continue indefinitely.

See also Question 75.

THE CASE FOR NOT RACKING

52. *I have been told that racking wines during the fermentation keeps them strong and healthy, because it adds oxygen needed by the yeast to keep things going. I tried this but without success. The reverse seemed true, for the wine seemed inclined to stick. What do you think about this?*

It is strange how this idea of "helping the fermentation by racking" persists, but it is always cropping up in some place or other. In order to answer it, one has to review the part air plays in the conversion of sugar to alcohol.

Oxygen is needed by the yeast at the start of a fermentation because the amount of yeast being added is insufficient to carry through a strong fermentation. In the presence of air, called an *aerobic* condition, yeast cells reproduce at their strongest because they can then secure the maximum of energy from the sugar, breaking this down to carbon dioxide and water. Air contains some 21% of oxygen, and when the surface of the must is in contact with air there is bound to be some available, but since carbon dioxide is being released the liquid should be stirred vigorously from time to time. This is our so-called "tumultuous fermentation", conducted in a pail covered with a cloth. Little alcohol is formed, but the yeast colonies are building up steadily.

The next stage is a change to *anerobic* conditions, when the must is transferred to a demijohn and air excluded by means of an air lock. The yeast's natural equipment allows it to live despite the absence of air, but cell-reproduction slows down to the extent that the number of cells produced roughly equals the number that die. And, further, the quantity of alcohol (an incompletely oxidised substance) increases steadily in the must.

There should thus be no call at all for a racking to introduce air in the middle of a fermentation. Perhaps the original aim was to encourage the yeast to produce more cells, but this is not necessary if the first stage of fermentation was conducted correctly with air present. What usually happens is that the must is racked off the lees, and this defeats the original object, because the dead cells on the bottom contain many resting viable cells as well as cells autolysing and releasing helpful nutrients. Doubtless you racked in this way, so that the net result was a decrease in cell population and a tendency for the wine to stick.

MILK SUGAR

53. *When I sweeten my wine, unless I drink it at once, it starts to ferment again. I have heard that a sugar called Milk Sugar can be used, which sweetens as ordinary grocer's sugar and yet remains stable. What is it and why does it not referment?*

Lactose is an animal sugar, not found in the vegetable kingdom. It can be obtained by the evaporation of whey from which the fat has been removed. Cow's milk contains about 4·5% of this, and human milk 7%. It is similar to sucrose and maltose in being a *disaccharide*, which merely means that it can be split into simpler sugars viz. glucose and galactose.

There are some yeasts that can ferment it after it has been degraded by them into its two unit sugars, but wine yeasts cannot do this because they do not contain the necessary enzyme called *lactase* to break it down. Therefore the fermenting enzymes of the wine yeast cannot get on with the job of converting it to alcohol, and it remains intact as lactose in the must or wine.

The value of this to winemakers is obvious, since it can be added as a sweetening agent without any fear of it starting up another fermentation. Use it just as you would any other sugar, stirring it into the wine. There are two points to bear in mind however. First, it is hard and dissolves with difficulty even in water; second, its sweetening power is only about one-third that of ordinary sugar, so that its use can be expensive. The first problem can be eased by warming up a little of the wine and stirring in the lactose before adding to the bulk, but the second remains.

See also Question 58.

READY FOR THE BOTTLE

54. *I am a beginner, and understand that wine should be kept some time in gallon containers before bottling. But how does one know when to bottle the wine? Is it after a fixed time?*

There is no fixed period, the indications of readiness for bottling being the state of clarity of the wine and the amount of deposit falling. If you wish to bottle early, then probably after the second racking is right if the deposit at that time is light. If it still has depth, then wait till the third. This assumes that the wine has then fallen clear. There is no point in bottling wine that may prove to be in need of fining, it is sheer waste of time.

Most winemakers keep their wine in bulk until it is fully matured. The advantage is that maturation seems to proceed better in bulk, and also cellarcraft can more easily be carried out. A bottled and capsuled wine is inclined to mature more slowly, so that it seems better not to rush this aspect of winemaking. Another point is that a bottle put down early will almost certainly need decanting, especially the reds. Against this, is that wine stored in bulk allows for constant sampling, with the result that when considered ready there is often enough only for one bottle! This, of course, is a very personal opinion!

EXCESS SULPHITE

55. *Through my own fault, there is an excess of sulphite in my wine. Is it possible to remove it easily?*

Aerating the wine by racking and dropping from a height should help to reduce the strength of the sulphite. Bring the wine into a warm room prior to this.

If it is really heavy in sulphite, you could try the addition of a little hydrogen peroxide, the bleach available at chemists. Test a small sample first in order to ascertain the proportion required for the bulk.

This is a very unusual question. Winemakers often find

an excess of one thing or another in their wine, but rarely sulphite. The fault seems an unnecessary one, and it is to be supposed that it corresponds with an excess of zeal in yourself.

SUGAR STICKERS
56. *What is the highest recommended gravity for a must when starting the fermentation to ensure that the amount of sugar present does not hold up a good start to this?*

When a must is too sweet, the addition of the yeast produces a process known as osmosis. This refers to the sucking out of the water content of the yeast cells by the denser solution of sugar in which they are placed. Two solutions of different densities or "thicknesses", separated by a membrane such as a cell wall, always endeavour to equalise their strength. As a result the dried up cells cannot continue activity, for they need to contain about 65% of water, and they are immobilised. At once the wine sticks, or does not even get under way, and dilution of the must is necessary for the fermentation to start.

There is little likelihood of this occurring with modern yeasts up to a gravity of 80. Nevertheless I still start my fermentation around 40, despite the knowledge that it is not essential, adding the remainder of the sugar when transferring the must to the demijohn, and certainly never have a non-starter.

It is when making a dessert type of wine, where the gravity needs to be beyond 100 in order to allow for residual sugar, that one can run into trouble. In such cases one should use a wine yeast of a variety that is acclimatised to a sugary environment and high alcohol level, such as a Sauternes, Port or Tokay. In addition the sugar should be "fed" in stages in order to ensure that the fermentation gets off to a good start, with no possibility of osmosis interfering with this.

TOO MUCH TANNIN
57. *There is too much tannin in my elderberry wine. It clings to the back of my teeth and the taste is rough and astringent. What can I do to remove it? Otherwise it seems a sound wine.*

Fining the wine will substantially reduce the tannin content, but the finings should be some form of protein: Bentonite, a montmorillonite or clay, is no use for this purpose.

The tannates in the wine have a negative electrical charge, and if we introduce particles of a substance containing a positive charge then an insoluble protein-tannin complex will be formed, and eventually gravitate to the bottom. The result is thus a reduction in tannin content.

The easiest fining agent to employ to this end is isinglass, available at wine counters in Boots. If it is in fibre form, break these down to a powder, and dissolve the amount recommended for fining in a cupful of water plus a pinch of tartaric acid. When set into a jelly, beat up in a jug of wine and add to the bulk. Should too much tannin be taken out from the wine in this way, it is simple to add more, the liquid form of tannin being the easier to use. Certainly do not remove all the tannin, or your wine will not clear.

Keep carefully to the recommended amount on the packet. It is easy to fine a second time if not enough tannin is removed at first, but an excess of isinglass can cause its own problem by leaving an "over-fining" haze.

See also Question 24.

ARTIFICIAL SWEETENERS
58. *Can I use saccharin safely as a sweetener to a finished wine? Presumably this would be unable to restart fermentation, and it has the advantages of being cheap and strong.*

These ersatz sweeteners can be used as you say, and they bring with them no problems of refermentation because they are sugar free.

The question is, although you do not mention it, whether they confer a detectable flavour of their own. In the end, this turns on the individual palate, and you must try them for yourself. I can detect their use to convert a dry to a sweet wine, but it is more subtle and less distinguishable where some sugar is already present. In any case, do not use it for competition wines, but only for your daily plonk. On the other hand, its employment may well suit the ladies who are on a calory-controlled diet, and miss their sweet wine.

There is another important point to keep in mind: the use

of saccharin will bring no body to the wine as does sugar, so that your sweetened wine is likely to seem peculiarly thin and unbalanced, if this artificial sweetener is used to saccharify a very dry wine into one with considerable sweetness.

See also Question 53.

MADERISED WINE

59. *What is meant when a wine is referred to as "maderised"? Is it another term for oxidised?*

The term "maderised" is sometimes loosely used for an oxidised wine, although this is better described as rancio-flavoured or sherry-like. Correctly it should be reserved for a different flavour peculiar to Madeira wine, and if you have tasted a Verdelho or Malmsey example of this you will know what is meant. If not, you have an excellent excuse to buy yourself a bottle of Amontillado Sherry and a bottle of Verdelho Madeira, and to have a marvellous evening comparing the two.

A curious method is employed in producing Madeira. It is placed in *estufas* or stoves for four or five months where it is warmed to a temperature of 120°F or so. As a result, there is a most distinctive caramel taste with all Madeiras, a cooked sugar taste, rather smoky in the case of Verdelho. This is what is inferred when a wine is referred to as "maderised", or at least it should be if correctly used.

If your wine acquires this flavour, the probable cause is storage over a period of time at too high a temperature, perhaps in a loft during summer. Sometimes an oxidised wine resembles this in flavour, but it is not exactly the same thing.

FLOWERS OF WINE

60. *A white skin has formed on the wine in my gallon jar. Is this the dreaded "Flowers of Wine"? Does it mean that I have been lax in some way?*

This white pellicle or skin used to be quite common in grandmother's day, and the term dates from then, although whether "flowers" refers to the little white islands that eventually join together to cover the surface of the wine, or whether it is a variant of "flour" in the sense of whiteness, is not certain.

Its appearance is unusual today for two reasons: we are more careful with hygiene, not allowing the wine must to stay in contact with the air, and sulphiting regularly, and further, our wines are innoculated with powerful wine yeasts which can reach an alcohol content that discourages this wild yeast.

For yeast it is, a wild genus known as *Candida mycoderma*. To multiply it needs plenty of air, and consequently when it is seen about in our time it is usually on the surface of some dregs of wine of low alcohol content that have been left at the bottom of an opened bottle for some time.

It need never bother a modern winemaker, and you should regard it as a warning to check up on your methods and tighten up your hygiene!

HELPING A MALO-LACTIC

61. *My wine contains predominantly malic acid. I should like to bring about a malo-lactic fermentation to soften the rough taste, and not leave this to happen by chance. How can I do this?*

When malic acid is strongly in evidence in a wine, this is likely to be rough and harsh, so that a secondary fermentation called malo-lactic is to be welcomed when it arrives some time after the main fermentation, an air-lock being fitted to allow the carbon dioxide gas formed to escape. The result is the conversion of much of the malic to the softer lactic acid, with a corresponding improvement to the wine.

This fermentation is however, as you say, a matter of chance, because you cannot easily obtain the *Lactobacilli fermenti* or *Bacterium gracile* needed for the change. If you are aiming at this taking place because your acid is mainly malic, start off at the beginning by avoiding the use of sulphite in the must, as *Lactobacilli* are sensitive to this. In its place you should rely on a high acid content to ward off bacterial attacks, and guard against oxidation by including six 50 mg. Vitamin C tablets. When the wine has finished fermenting, store in a warm place to encourage development, for *Lactobacilli* are thermophilic. Also you could add a little yeast nutrient at this stage, but only if your wine is now quite dry or you will start up your original fermentation. There is no need to bother about any need for the presence of air, for this has no effect on a malo-lactic fermentation. Fit an air-lock when the wine starts to bubble.

You may be unlucky in having no *Lactobacilli* present in the must from the start, so that it must still be somewhat dicey, but at least if you carry out these instructions you are doing all you can to bring about the conversion of acid that you want.

See also Questions 21 and 62.

FOR BETTER OR WORSE

62. *I always understood that a malo-lactic fermentation was a good thing in smoothing out a wine, but now I have been told by a wine judge that the thickness at the bottom of my bottle is due to lactic-acid bacilli infection. How can this be?*

There is a considerable number of species of *Lactobacilli*, and many of these are undesirable in wine. The thickness or viscosity in your wine is probably dextran, a glucose polysaccharide, plus a gummy slime, formed by *Leuconostoc mesenterrides* often found in association with *Lactobacilli*.

The desirable malo-lactic fermentation is produced by other species, such as *Lactobacilli fermenti*, *Lactobacilli brevis*, *Micrococcus malolacticus*, and others.

So this genus is a very mixed bunch, including both friends and foes of the winemaker.

See also Quesions 21 and 61.

CURING OXIDATION

63. *My wine has become oxidised, probably because I had drawn off a bottle for show purposes and did not replace it because I had sweetened it. Will the addition of Campden tablets be of any benefit in removing the oxidised flavour?*

Campden tablets are not recommended for this trouble; they bring their own problem if used heavily with a finished wine. You could try ascorbic acid, which should not affect the flavour too badly, although you must realise that once this "back oxidation" has been allowed to develop there is really nothing one can do to reverse the process to its original state.

A drastic dosage is needed, up to ten 100 mg. Vitamin C tablets (ascorbic acid), or proportionately if your tablets are smaller in content. This amount is safe for the drinker and good for the common cold, so if you still do not like the flavour of your wine, you can tell yourself that it is doing you good.

See also Questions 44 and 45.

FLOATING YEAST

64. *My primary fermentation is going well, but there is a layer of yeast on top of the must. Why is this and should I scoop it off?*

Some types of yeast tend to come to the top more than others, especially at the start of the "tumultuous" fermentation. As you probably know, there "top" and "bottom" yeasts used in brewing beer, the first being the British ale yeast and the second the Continental lager yeast. Wine yeasts are closely related to the British top yeast, *Saccharomyces cerevisiae*, which is considered to be the parent type of all culture yeasts. No doubt the bottom lager yeasts were developed from them by genetical segregation.

As there is little difference of density between the cells of the two types, this is not the cause of one sinking and the other rising. The cause is due to the buds not separating from the parent cells at this time of intense aerobic reproduction, so that chains of cells are formed that trap bubbles of carbon dioxide, then being carried to the surface of the must. The proportion of cells performing in this way varies somewhat according to the type of wine yeast being used.

Certainly do not scoop these off, but stir the must regularly to disperse them in the liquid and to provide them with ample oxygen.

MATURING IN CASK

65. *Would it improve my wine if I invested in wooden casks in which to store it, instead of using glass demijohns and carboys?*

Certainly, but with certain reservations. First the good

points; wood is porous, which means that the wine can breathe. Therefore it has access to atmospheric oxygen, and trace oxidation, an essential part of the maturing process, can proceed regularly. In addition, the wood acts as a filter. Some commercial cellarmen abroad claim that the local oak regulates the tannin, absorbing it where it exists in excess, or contributing it to the wine where there is a deficiency. Certainly, wine that has been in the wood has a recognisable quality which, where correctly controlled, is to be associated with vinosity.

Against these points, one must recognise that there is an inherent danger of over-oxidation for amateurs. Home winemakers tend to go in for three-gallon size casks, or even smaller because of storage problems, instead of the large $4\frac{1}{2}$'s and 6's. As a result, the area surface of wood in contact with wine is proportionately greater than with the increasingly larger casks. Therefore oxidation may proceed at too fast a rate, and although this chemical reaction is essential to the ageing process, spoilage will result where it goes too far too quickly. Small casks, therefore, are dangerous unless very carefully watched, and white wine is better not put into them at all.

Evaporation is a characteristic of cask-matured wines. Normally, one might expect the smaller water molecule to pass through the wood more quickly than that of alcohol, which is much larger, so that the wine increases in strength. In fact this turns on the surrounding humidity of the air. Water evaporation will be less in damp surroundings, but faster in dry conditions such as prevail in Spain, where Sherry increases in alcohol content during maturation. But do not let this delude you that the same will happen in this fog-stricken country, unless the air in your cellar is very dry for some reason or other.

See also Question 36.

A USE FOR EVERYTHING
66. *My five gallons of apple wine are badly oxidised, owing to my carelessness in making it. I would be prepared to throw away one gallon, but must five gallons be wasted because of this disagreeable taint?*

Sometimes one can redeem a wine that is not too badly affected by adding ascorbic acid, but where the strong rancio taste has settled in, there is little help to be had from this source. It can certainly render a table wine unacceptable, particularly apple, which one would expect to be crisp and fresh.

However, do not despair. First try sweetening and fortifying a trial amount, plus acid addition, in order to achieve an oloroso-type sherry. You will, of course, need more body for this, so some glycerine added, or C.G.J., or the juice of dried bananas obtained by simmering them in water, can help in this respect.

If you do not like the result, try instead a strong vermouth-flavour additive, to cover up the defect. Should a stronger cover still be called for, you could try the wine as the base of a spiced punch, including such flavours as cinnamon.

Finally it might come in handy for cooking, if the flavours it has to associate with are not too delicate.

Still unhappy? Use it as a warning to beginners at your Club, or for training would-be judges. Five gallons should last you a lifetime.

See also Questions 44, 45 and 63.

ACETIC WINE

67. *Is there anything to be done with a wine that has acquired a taste of vinegar. Could I blend it or add a flavouring to disguise it?*

No. Once *Acetobacter* have gained entry into a wine and brought about the partial oxidation of alcohol to acetic acid, the wine is ruined. The cause is always the admission of air to the wine over a period, because the bacteria causing the change are aerobic and need free oxygen for the reaction. Some types of these bacteria, known as *Acetomonas*, will continue the oxidation process to its ultimate end, converting the acetic acid into carbon dioxide and water, so that if a wine is attacked in this way, we are back where we started, but of course such neglect is very unlikely.

More usually the wine is acetified, with a resulting sharp taste that one associates with vinegar, and where this is present the wine is useless as a beverage. All you can do is to punch a few holes in the cork and serve it with your fish and chips

A CURIOUS HAZE

68. *I had a persistent haze in gooseberry wine and tried all the usual clearing methods including a pectin test. Then by some odd chance, I tested it for starch, and this showed positive. A starch enzyme was added, and it cleared. How could this trouble originate with a non-cereal wine?*

This can happen where glucose is used instead of grocer's sugar, but presumably this was not so in your case or you would have mentioned it, as it is a departure from the more normal use of sugar (sucrose).

Therefore I can only imagine that starch has been used as a binding agent in something used by you in making up the must, or later. Perhaps the Campden tablets contained sufficient of this to produce the haze. It is certainly unusual.

See also Question 39.

ALCOHOL CHECKS

69. *Is there an easy method of checking the alcohol content of a wine other than that of a hydrometer and conversion tables?*

As you know, the initial reading of your hydrometer can give you the potential alcohol content of your must, provided that all the sugar is converted to alcohol and the wine is quite dry after the fermentation. The second method when the wine is finished is to take the difference between the initial and final gravity readings, and then to divide this figure by a variable factor. Unfortunately, the result of arriving at the alcohol content by the hydrometer is interfered with by such things as the dissolved solids other than sugar, the amount of alcohol present and the temperature of the liquid, so that the assessment is often badly out. Further, the initial gravity must be known; one cannot just pick up an unknown wine and arrive at its alcohol content.

Perhaps this is why you are looking for an alternative method. Of course, your Club could invest in a Wine Refractometer for the use of members: its use needs no scientific knowledge at all, and the test takes about a minute, but they are expensive. If you are prepared to take a little trouble, then the "evaporation test" might be what you are looking for. Its use involves the hydrometer, but there is no need to know the initial reading of the must, and the result is reasonably accurate.

Take the gravity of the wine being tested, and then measure at least 200 mls. of it into a flask, and simmer until it has been reduced to half this amount, in order to evaporate the alcohol content. Add distilled water to bring it up to the original quantity, and at 60°F take its gravity again. Subtract the first reading from the second, and from the following table ascertain the alcohol content of the wine. You may need more than 200 mls. in order for your hydrometer to float, and for greater accuracy a short range hydrometer is helpful.

Conversion Table

Increase in Degrees	Alcohol Content
10	7·2
12	8·8
13	9·7
14	10·5
15	11·4
16	12·3
17	13·2
18	14·1
19	15·1
20	16·0
21	17·0
22	18·0

See also Questions 25, 78 and 82.

STUCK AGAIN

70. *What is the best method to overcome a stuck fermentation?* Presumably by this you mean a fermentation which has started but then come to a halt. This is not the same thing as a fermentation that will not start, and needs different treatment. But first check over the balance of your must along the lines of that suggested for Question 23. If you are happy about this, then try in turn the following methods.

1. Revive it with a "booster". Crush a 3 mg. tablet of Vitamin B, and mix with half a level teaspoon of di-ammonium phosphate and the tip of a teaspoon of magnesium sulphate, the last particularly if your water is at all soft. Dissolve in a little warm water and add to the must. Stir the must vigorously prior to this.

2. If there is still no movement, add a fresh yeast. Use a strong type of the sort that is sprinkled on the surface of the must, because it is dangerous to leave the latter at this stage while a starter bottle is prepared. Put the pail, into which you have transferred the must from the demijohn, in a warm place to encourage a new start.

3. Take a pint of must and if the gravity is over 40°, dilute it below this figure. Put into a wine bottle, add a little granulated yeast, plug with cotton wool, and again keep warm. When it is fermenting strongly, add to the remainder of the must in a covered pail, and transfer again to the demijohn when the fermentation is well under way.

4. If all three methods have failed, add the lifeless must gradually in separate amounts to another must that is working well in its pail. You will have to accept the combination of flavours that results, but check up on the balance of acid, tannin, etc., before fitting an air-lock.

See also Question 23.

VERY DRY WINES

71. *Must a dry wine by definition contain no sugar at all, or is a small amount of residual sugar permissible? If so, what amount can be permitted before wine judges disqualify the wine as "out of class" as a dry entry?*

A dry wine can contain a small amount of residual sugar, and indeed many would be improved by this. Totally dry wines, where all sugar has been ferementented out, can often be harsh, whereas a trifle of residual sugar would have helped to smooth this out, without the wine moving out of a dry classification.

From the point of view of palate, the sugar present should not draw attention to itself; if there is sufficient to do this, then the wine will rightly be regarded as a medium-dry, and be disqualified when entered in a dry class. If, however, the residual sugar approaches the threshold of recognition in the palate without passing it, then it is unlikely that it will be turned down as dry. The palate may be aware in a vague way that the wine's smoothness is associated with sugar, but the impression is too blurred for the mental response to signal "sweet".

If you wish to conduct a test to determine the amount of sugar present, then use the Clinitest for this purpose. The hydrometer is too strongly influenced by other factors to be of any use for such a delicate test. I suggest that you limit your residual sugar to 1% if you are entering your wine in the dry class of a competition, although you can go up to 2% with some wines; much depends on other constituents of the wine, such as body and alcohol content. If, however, the wine is for your own consumption, such a fine distinction is of no great consequence.

See also Questions 41, 72 and 73.

SUGAR TESTING

72. *I have several times done badly in competition because my dry wines were judged to be "out of class" on account of sweetness. Yet my hydrometer was well below 0° with all of them. Should I get another hydrometer?*

Forget the hydrometer! It is an excellent instrument, but it is really of little use in determining a dry wine. On the one hand, we have unfermentables pushing up the reading, and on the other alcohol pulling it down. The instrument tells the truth as regards the gravity of the wine, but it cannot distinguish between the various factors affecting it. If it was dealing with a mixture of water and sugar, then we could rely on it for indicating the amount of sugar present, but wine is a very complex substance indeed.

Therefore test for a dry wine with a Clinitest Outfit. A small outlay will give you some thirty or so tests, and the results are accurate as well as easy to obtain. The change in colour of a wine after adding a Clinitest tablet is matched with a chart to determine the amount of sugar. Another proprietary product is Dextrocheck, where a tape is dipped into the wine, resulting in a colour change.

Such tests will be sensitive up to 2% residual sugar,

although the readings can be taken up to double this amount by diluting the wine with an equal quantity of distilled water. At this point a warning must be given. The tests are both specific only for *dextrose*. Thus, while they are successful for residual sugar in a finished wine, they will not react to sucrose, the grocer's sugar normally used for winemaking. Therefore do not attempt to increase the sugar content with sugar syrup and expect the test outfit to indicate this addition; it *might* show a small increase because of some slight inversion of the sugar during boiling, but this could mislead you to the extent that you add far too much sugar. Employ the test for residual sugar only; for increasing sugar content by adding sugar syrup, rely on tables in good wine books. Roughly two teaspoons of syrup will raise one gallon of wine 0·25%.

See also Questions 41, 71 and 73.

SERIOUS DOUBTS

73. *I recently tested an old well-matured wine with a Clinitest Outfit. It showed the wine to be completely dry, yet I can distinctly detect a slight sweetness on the palate. I always thought these outfits were infallible. What is the reason?*

The Clinitest and the Dextrocheck are the best methods we have for testing residual sugar in our wines, and if these indicate no sugar in your wine they are correct—always remembering that the sugar they refer to is dextrose. Unfortunately, from the point of view of ascertaining sugar content, wines can also contain other ingredients that bring sweetness, and these the tests cannot detect.

The two main ingredients referred to are non-fermentable pentose sugars and of course glycerine. The amounts of these vary from wine to wine, but it has been estimated that an old claret could contain 0·7 gms. of pentose sugar, with a sweetness factor about half that of fermentable sugars. and about 10 gms. of glycerine, which is half as sweet again as glucose and fructose. What has happened is that the flavour of tannin and acid has softened out in your matured wine, so allowing these sweetness factors to become noticeable. It all goes to show that the palate's decision is final,

See also Questions 41, 71 and 72.

GLYCERINE

74. *Since glycerine is said to be produced naturally during fermentation, is there anything against introducing it to a wine that needs more body? Sugar I know can thicken a wine, but it sweetens it at the same time.*

As you say, glycerine is produced during fermentation, and in times of shortage sugar has been diverted from the normal fermentation path to produce glycerine at the expense of alcohol.

As it mixes well with water and alcohol in any proportion, its introduction to wine helps to smooth out harshness and to increase body. Unfortunately, although it is colourless and odourless, it does have some slight distinctive flavour, and this may be detected if employed to excess. Further, it is certainly sweet, and here again you must be careful if you want to keep a wine dry. As a maximum, I should say two fluid ounces to a gallon, although this amount will turn a dry wine into a medium usually, the final sweetness depending on the degree of original dryness. If winemakers use it at all, they use it in much smaller quantities.

From the "moral" point of view, some purists regard it as artificial, although one could argue all day about which additives are natural and which are not. No competition rules debar it specifically, although in a very wide approach it could be regarded as an alcohol addition, because curiously enough it is chemically a trihydric alcohol. Certainly it can help out a wine that is below par.

LATE CLOUDING

75. *I put a wine away to mature, and watched it clear quickly until it was star bright. When I looked at it recently, I was amazed to find it cloudy again. I cannot understand this behaviour at all.*

It is easy enough to see that wine is "working" during the fermentation period, but it is more difficult to realise that this action continues, although in different directions, after the fermentation, when the wine appears placid and still, in its jar. We speak loosely of the wine being "finished" when we rack it off its lees, but it is only half so, and during maturation it continues "working" although much less convincingly so to the eye.

Consequently, winemakers are frequently surprised when something unexpectedly visible occurs as a result of such post-fermentative changes, apart from the usual fall-out of sediment. In your case, what has happened, to speak in a very general way, is that substances which were previously dissolved and therefore invisible have through chemical change become precipitated out of solution to produce a visible haze. What the particular reaction is depends on the type of wine, its ingredients and its balance, but I would suggest specific reactions between tannins and proteins, between acetaldehyde and anthocyanin pigments—although these should drop, or between acetaldehyde and tannins previously in solution.

Of course, the haze could be a secondary fermentation, but this cause is only too obvious with the gas produced causing the cork to pop, and you do not mention this.

See also Question 51.

SECTION III
FUSEL OIL

76. *What exactly is fusel oil? I know that it is a bad thing to have in wine, but how is it formed when the ingredients contain no oil at the start?*

It is not an oil in the usual sense of the word, but an alcohol or more correctly a mixture of alcohols. Probably the word "fusel" with its echo of "diesel" emphasises the idea of oil, but really the name means *worthless*, although one cannot condemn it outright as such in a wine or spirit.

Fusel oil is a collective expression for a mixture of heavy alcohols, mainly isomers of amyl and butyl alcohol, together with some fatty acids and their esters. It does not arise from the fermentation of sugar to alcohol, but is formed separately during fermentation from the assimilation by the yeast of amino acids from the protein of the ingredients in the must.

Its content therefore depends largely on the type of material being fermented, and such ingredients as grain, potatoes, beetroots, bring the likelihood of a larger than usual amount of fusel oil into the finished wine. Incidentally, the fiery brandy called "marc" in France and "grappa" in Italy contains a higher proportion too, and these alcohols can be detected in the bouquet.

Normally, fusel oil is present only in minute quantities in our wines, and they present no danger to the drinker, while contributing to the flavour and bouquet as the wine matures.

See also Questions 12 and 46.

TITRATION QUERY
77. *I have started titrating my musts for acid content, and find it quite a simple process. But why is acid level expressed in parts per thousand sulphuric acid, when one is dealing with citric, tartaric and malic acids in winemaking?*

This question comes up from time to time, and it is a very natural one to ask. The answer is that it is a convention that has become established as the norm by time and custom, so that it is now current practice when measuring acidity in parts per thousand to state this in terms of sulphuric acid. If there is a distinct advantage in changing a traditional practice, then I am in favour of doing so, but this one has points in its favour and therefore a claim to its retention. A convention is not necessarily bad because it is old.

First its use simplifies our calculations. If 5 mls. of wine are taken as the sample for testing, (provided that the sodium hydroxide is a decinormal solution, as usually the case), the amount of alkali added in mls. is the acidity of the wine in p.p.t. sulphuric, without any further calculations or references to tables being necessary. If 10 mls. of wine are used, one simply divides the amount of alkali added in mls. by 2, and so on. These results are accurate enough for our purpose.

Secondly, it is easy to change p.p.t. sulphuric to p.p.t. citric, tartaric or malic, by multiplying by 1·43, 1·34 and 1·53 respectively, but tables supplied with your titration outfit relieve you even of this burden, assuming that you wish to know.

Thirdly, there is little need for such conversion, for again a titration set will have information on the amount of acid to add to your must, equating ounces of all three acids with parts per thousand sulphuric acid in a gallon of must.

Lastly, even if we did talk in terms of, say p.p.t. citric acid, the need for the conversion to other acids where they were used could still arise.

It is worth noting that when we speak of acid content not in parts per thousand, but in percentage, then it *is* usual to do so in terms of the particular fruit acid used.

SWEET OR DESSERT

78. *I entered recently in a dessert class at a competition and came nowhere. The judge said later that my wine was really out of class because it was not a dessert wine. Afterwards I tested its gravity and found it was 28, so what was he talking about?*

There is little doubt that the judge was correct in what he said. A sweet wine, which is so often a dry or medium wine sweetened up with sugar syrup, is not necessarily a dessert wine because of its sugar content, and this would be what the judge had in mind. You say nothing about other characteristics of your wine.

Three qualities are necessary for a wine to qualify for a dessert class. First, it must have body, or if you like thickness or viscosity, of that palpable nature that allows one almost to chew it in the mouth. Secondly, it must have a mouth-filling flavour and fruitiness, for remember that it will be drunk when a whole range of flavours of food have been enjoyed, and the palate is far from fresh. Thirdly, it must have sufficient alcohol to support this sweetness and this flavour, so that the fumes can carry these to the olfactory senses at the back of the mouth, so avoiding the feeling that one is sipping a sweet cordial.

Really, these qualities can come only in a wine that is intended from the start to be a dessert wine, employing ample quantities of ingredients, a potent and suitable yeast, and probably sugar "fed" to the must in stages. Dessert wines of quality are not arrived at by doctoring up wines that you have entered in another class, nor are they to be equated with sweet wines that lack other essential characteristics. Treat yourself to a half bottle of a good Sauternes or Barsac, and follow a glass of this with a sample of your own. You will soon see what the judge was talking about.

FIXED OR VARIABLE

79. *In an early wine book I learned that the amount of alcohol in a finished wine could be determined by subtracting the final reading of the hydrometer from the original reading, and then dividing the result by 7·4. I have now been told that this is not an accurate method. Why is this?*

The division by a fixed factor such as 7·4 or 7·36 is not altogether accurate for all musts, and modern wine books usually suggest a factor graduated to the initial gravity of the must, thus allowing for individual differences.

The explanation is that a fixed factor would be in order if the volume of the must remained constant throughout the fermentation. But because the volume of alcohol produced is less than the volume taken up by the sugar before the conversion, the final Specific Gravity is heavier *than if this had not been the case*. Graded factors are therefore used, and these are decided by the gravity of the must at the start.

Thus one authority suggests, for example:

Corrected Initial Gravity	Graded Factor
80	7·45
90	7·41
100	7·37 etc.

Remember to deduct some 5 to 7 degrees from your initial reading to allow for unfermentable solids, according to the body of the must, in order to obtain the corrected sugar gravity. Also remember to deduct this same figure from your final reading too, because these solids are to a large extent still present in the finished wine.

See also Questions 25, 69 and 82.

JAPANESE SAKÉ

80. *Is there a recipe for Saké? Can I make it from brown rice?*

No. It is impossible to make this at home because the moulds necessary are not easily available in this country, although the Taka-diastase method of starch saccharification is manufactured by Parke-Davis.

The feature of sake is that the starch in the basic ingredient of rice is converted to maltose sugar by the mould called

Aspergillus oryzae. Only after this conversion is it possible to continue with fermentation by a yeast culture. In the Japanese process, both reactions proceed together, the yeast fermenting the maltose as soon as it is formed by the mould, so that the mould is not inhibited by the malt sugar's presence. In this way, an alcohol content of 20–22% is reached, although this is diluted for bottling.

Rice wine made by home winemakers is certainly not saké, although sometimes called by this name in recipes, because the alcohol is derived from the sucrose introduced into the must and not from the rice's conversion to maltose. The only role of the rice in such a wine is to flavour the liquid and confer some body.

CAMPDEN TABLETS

81. *What is the composition of Campden Tablets, and what is their strength? Are they safe, and what maximum limit do you recommend?*

The basic ingredient of these tablets is potassium metabisulphite. Sulphurous acid is a weak dibasic acid, and it forms two series of salts: sulphites, the normal salts, and the acid salts or bisulphites. Many of the bisulphites of alkaline metals, such as potassium and sodium, are hydrated, and the *meta* forms designate compounds derived from, or metameric with, those to the names of which the term "meta" is prefixed. Thus metabisulphite may be regarded as the anhydrous form of bisulphite, and is the convenient solid form for the use of winemakers.

Each tablet contains 7 grains of the salt, i.e. about 0·45 gms. One tablet conveys 50 parts per million sulphur dioxide to one gallon of liquid, the usual quantity being used consisting of two tablets to a gallon, although where the fruit shows signs of decay more may be called for.

This is a perfectly safe amount and well below the level permitted for continental vignerons. France's limit is as high as 450 p.p.m.

See also Question 18.

HYDROMETER TABLES

82. *Why do tables that convert hydrometer readings of the* *must before fermentation into percentages of potential alcohol, not always agree in the figures that they give?*

There are several reasons for this variation, although if the tables are up to date the variations are usually slight, at the maximum perhaps 1%.

The main trouble arises from the fact that the must contains not only dissolved sugar which will eventually ferment out, or most of it where the amount is high, but also dissolved unfermentable substances, as well as suspended undissolved solids. As it is impossible, except by chemical analysis, for us to separate the quantity of fermentable sugar from the other non-fermentable matter, the hydrometer reading will include both of these together. In other words, the gravity will be shown as higher than for the true sugar content.

Consequently, an allowance must be made, and the question is how much? Early tables in winemaking books were based on continental ones which took grape juice as the normal medium, and consequently 10 was allowed for the presence of the unfermentable substances. Our fruits are generally lighter, and 5–7 deduction would be closer to the correct figure, so that these early tables forecast a lower percentage of potential alcohol than later ones.

It would be helpful if the calculators of potential alcohol tables both in books and on hydrometers would always say whether they are working with corrected figures, and if so what allowance they are making to arrive at the true sugar content. This allowance figure, it should always be remembered, must be deducted by you both from the initial gravity and the final gravity as well, if you are checking on the alcohol content by deducting one figure from the other and dividing by a graded factor, in order to ascertain the drop after fermentation. This is because to a large extent the unfermentables are still present in the finished wine as they were at the beginning in the must, although it is true that suspended solids are less in evidence, having gravitated out.

See also Questions 25, 69 and 78.

WINE YEAST FLAVOUR

83. *Is it beneficial to leave fermented wine on the lees for one or two months before racking in order for the wine yeast to confer its particular local-wine flavour on the wine?*

This idea of leaving wine on the settled yeast without racking seems to have originated from one of the pioneers of the home-winemaking movement. I can clearly remember statements to this effect during public lectures, and I have discussed the matter with her. But I do not go along with it.

It may well be that, among other important influences such as differences in the soil, the positioning of the vines and the variety of the grape, the subtle variations of flavour and bouquet that distinguish one commercial wine from another may also be determined by the strain of wine yeast from a particular district. It has been established that different wine yeasts have different systems of enzymes, and where these systems are similar they exist in varying strengths and quantities. Such variations in enzymic make-up can have quite marked effects on the resulting fermentation, and its contents, and in this way the flavour and bouquet of the wine can be affected.

Even so, yeasts are modified by their environment and it is questionable for how long, say, a Burgundy yeast placed in quite a different must from the one in which it was propagated will persist in the characteristics of its type before becoming modified by its surrounding medium. The claim, therefore, of a certain continental yeast being able to confer the properties of a continental wine on a home-made product is open to some doubt.

Further, assuming that such yeasts do affect flavour of wines made at home by their individualised conduct of the fermentation, I cannot feel that this is enhanced by leaving the wine on the dead yeast for a month or so before the first racking. Pulp debris forms a large part of the lees, and this together with autolysing yeast cells is likely to do considerable harm in giving rise to undesirable off-flavours in the wine.

See also Question 17.

GYPSUM ADDITION

84. *I believe abroad, especially in Spain, gypsum is added to the fermenting musts. What is the purpose of this, and what is the chemical effect?*

This process is common in hot climates where there is a deficiency of acid in the must, and at the same time gypsum is available cheaply. It is often referred to as "plastering".

Grape juice in warm climates contains tartaric acid in the form of a potassium salt, potassium bitartrate. Gypsum is chemically known as crystalline hydrated calcium sulphate. When gypsum is added to the grape must, these two salts inter-react, and an interchange of elements takes place. Consequently they reappear as calcium tartrate, which is precipitated out, and as potassium sulphate, which remains in solution together with free tartaric acid into the bargain.

As a result, two benefits are derived. First the acidity of the wine is increased, the tartaric acid now being free of potassium. Secondly, the crystallising out of the potassium tartrate in the from of argol at the bottom of bottles is avoided. It is harmless enough, but such deposits often cause the uninformed public to return bottles of wine where this has taken place.

The drawback is that the sulphate remaining in the wine may react with the tartaric acid, replacing part of this with sulphuric acid, an undesirable state of affairs. Therefore in Provence, calcium phosphate is used instead of calcium sulphate (gyspum), so that if any tartaric acid is replaced it will be by phosphoric and not sulphuric acid.

An obvious query is, why not add tartaric acid as amateurs do with their wines? The answer is one of economics: refined tartaric acid in bulk is too expensive for profit-making producers to employ in this way.

FORTIFYING DESSERTS

85. *How does one make a dessert wine by fortification? How do I know how much spirit to add?*

Presumably you are referring to dessert wines made by fortifying with a suitable spirit when the amount of sugar remaining has reached the level required. A neutral spirit, such as Vodka, is used for a Sauternes type, and Brandy for a Port. Remember however that if you intend to enter for a competition with such a wine, the regulations may forbid fortified wines, so study them carefully.

In order to calculate the amount of spirit required, use the Pearson Square:

```
    A                    D
              C
    B                    E
```

Ascertain the alcohol content of the wine at the stage when the residual sugar content is right for the type of wine you desire. This done by ascertaining the drop in gravity and referring to tables. Put the alcohol content figure at B. At C write the alcohol content that you require, and at D the difference between the two. At A goes the alcohol content of the spirit you are using, and at E the difference between A and C. The proportion of D to E is the proportion of spirit to wine for your purpose.

Say that your wine has reached 12% alcohol content, and you require 18%. You are using Vodka of 70° proof, i.e. 40% alcohol. Then your figures are:

```
   40                    6
              18
   12                    22
```

So you need 6 volumes of Vodka to 22 of wine, i.e. just about ¼. Obviously it pays to let your wine reach a higher alcohol content than this, because of the cost of the Vodka.

A STABILIZER

86. *Our Club shop has for sale a commercial stabilizer to check the refermentation of wine. I notice that the small print refers to "benzoate" as the main constituent. What is this, and is it safe to use?*

Wines, (like winemakers), do need stabilizing from time to time, especially when they are not quite dry and there is a rise in temperature. No matter how bright your wine, there are sure to be a few yeast cells knocking around, anxious to start working again (unlike winemakers), for we do not use the powerful pressure filters that commercial firms have at their disposal.

A food or drink preservative and corrosion inhibitor that has been in use for a very long time, and is frequently employed with fruit juices and drinks, is benzoic acid. It occurs in natural resins and in the gum "benzoin" from the tree *Styrax benzoin*, hence its name, but commercially it is synthetically produced in the form of water-soluble sodium benzoate.

It is quite safe, being non-toxic to drinkers, and has legal backing. Although successful enough in soft drinks, it is not always so effective where yeasts and nutrients are already in the wine, and cannot be guaranteed to inhibit refermentation every time.

See also Question 42.

SPACE AGE
87. *I read in a Science Fiction novel of a chemist establishing the age of wine with a Geiger Counter. Is this imagination or is there any truth behind it?*

It appears that this is really possible, although there does not seem to be any report of its being used in this way that I can discover. Tritium, or heavy hydrogen, formed by atoms colliding with cosmic rays, is absorbed by the vine from rain water taken in by its roots, and so finds its way eventually into the wine. There it steadily decreases, and since the rate of decrease over the years can be worked out in tables, the amounts registered on the counter can be expressed in terms of age. By the end of the century all National Judges no doubt will carry one around with them.

COPYING COMMERCIALS
88. *Several committees members of our Club are interested in commercial wine, and as a result a considerable amount of time this year is being given up to tastings of wines from famous districts abroad, and to lectures about them. I think this is a waste of time. We want individuality not standardisation of flavours.*

Once a winemaker has established himself as competent in the field of home winemaking, he can do a lot worse than getting to know as much as he can about Continental wines.

First, we need a norm or standard to set against the wines we are producing, and this is just what professionally-made wine can provide for us. It can broaden our horizons and get us outside self-conceived ideas of what wine types should be. I have been to judge at small club competitions where the same defect or excess runs through nearly all entries, and it is only too clear that they are groping in the dark towards what they think constitutes a dry table or a sweet dessert, so that they are moving in circles inside their little group without any clear lead in the right direction. Amateur winemaking after all has only been in existence, in its modern approach, for a couple of decades, whereas professional vignerons have a tradition extending back for centuries. There is no loss of face in studying their products for our own advantage.

Secondly, there is little reason to fear loss of individuality in so doing. From time to time we set out to produce a wine as close as possible to a certain commercial variety, and it is good fun in testing our winemaking ability in this way; some clubs have competitions along these lines, and remarkable results can be achieved. But at best, such wines are only imitations and copies of the real things. They are as bogus as margarine is to butter, despite the fact that one may prefer the former! The *real* reason for getting to know commercial wines is to understand the balance of ingredients, to recognise the levels of acid, tannin, fruit, sugar, alcohol and all that goes to make a wine supremely suitable for a certain practical purpose.

Thirdly, we can achieve this desirable balance with practice, and still preserve to ourselves, as we wish, that whole variety of flavours that distinguishes wines made from ingredients other than the grape. We select the best of two worlds, the professional and the amateur, with no loss of individuality in the process.

CLEANING A CASK

89. *I have been recommended to clean my cask with a piece of chain. Will rolling the cask around with this inside be sufficient? It smells badly.*

Get about four feet of chain and a couple of pounds of silver sand. Put them in the cask with a little water, and after having bunged it up, roll it about. This will remove the deposits that are often quite thick in a wine cask.

In your case, as the cask smells unpleasant, you will need still to disinfect it. Some use sulphur matches, but these are not recommended for amateurs as they can cause side-flavours. Fill the cask with a hypochlorite solution, say 5 ounces of Parazone to ten gallons of water, and leave it for a day. Then wash it out with a 2% sulphur dioxide solution, consisting of 5 ounces of Sodium metabisulphite in one gallon of water. Finally, swill and wash it thoroughly with a hose.

PLASTIC ADVICE

90. *To what extent are plastic vessels used for winemaking safe? If there is any danger, how does this arise in their manufacture?*

The danger in the use of plastics for winemaking lies in the additives used in manufacture. These are used as antioxidants with polythene and polypropylene to avoid breakdown, and as lubricants with polyvinylchloride to avoid sticking, and also as colouring pigments. Phenols, lead carbonate and sulphate, cadmium sulphide and lead chromate, are examples of these additives.

The manufacturers observe that the heavy metal components are well encapsulated, but for our purpose they have to be able to stand up against alcohol, acids and the fermentation process in general.

Plastics in some form seem indispensable to us, so until manufacturers label their products as safe from toxic materials, or suitable for winemaking processes, we should take certain precautions.

1. Use only white plastic containers, avoiding strong colours.

2. Avoid conducting the whole of the fermentation in plastic, always transferring the must to a glass container after the first stage.

3. Avoid storing for long periods in plastic containers, even after the fermentation has finished.

On the whole, this care is not so inconvenient for us. It is beermakers who seem to run the greatest risks, fermenting in dustbins that are not intended in any way at all to be used for domestic food or drink. Fortunately there is a general awareness of this danger, and beer is now brewed in polythene bags acting as liners inside the rigid dustbins.

JUDGE BASHING

91. *What happens when a judge suspects a wine entered in an amateur show as being a commercial product, put into another bottle? I know someone who boasts that he has got away with such a trick.*

This question must be answered personally, as different judges react differently in such a case.

Fortunately, this form of cheating is rare nowadays. Partly, because there seems such little satisfaction to be derived from such practice, except for pot-hunters and those desirous of being "one-up" on the judge, and partly because wine judges in general have a very real knowledge of commercial as well as amateur wines.

When a judge does suspect a wine on the showbench of being a commercial wine entered as an amateur product, he has a choice of two things: he can accept it and judge it on its merits against the other entries, or he can reject it as out of class. The practice of marking it down seems an irresolute compromise.

Some judges throw it out at once, and they are entitled to do so, but I do not go along with this, on the grounds that however strong my conviction is that it is not genuinely produced at home, I cannot *demonstrate* that this is so, any more than one can *prove* wine has been fortified, without going to a great deal of fuss and bother. There are some clubs whose members specialise in copying commercial types, and their results can be very convincing indeed. Thus there is always the possibility that it is genuine, so that the judge who rejects it as a fake is sticking his neck out. I know a judge who claims to finish off such wines for lunch and leave the empty bottle as a warning! This seems hazardous to me.

I accept all wines that are in my class and judge them as they come. If my suspicions are strong enough to amount to a certainty, then I make a note of the suspected wine and later ask the Convenor for information from the Club Secretary concerning the entrant. He seldom turns up to Judges-at-the-Bar sessions! If the answer confirms my suspicions, I can raise the matter at a Regional Judges' Meeting, or at the Annual Convention, so that we can see whether the practice is being repeated elsewhere.

Fortunately this shoddy practice is declining, and the formation of a Black List of Competitors is hardly necessary.

THE LITTLE EXTRA
92. My wine book informs me that a sterilizing solution for containers and equipment can be made by crushing Campden tablets and adding ½ oz. of citric acid. What purpose does the acid addition serve?

Sulphite efficiency in the liquid it is added to, is controlled by the acidity of this latter. Incidentally, this is another reason why it is so important to get your acid level right when balancing the must. Normally in an acidic must 100 p.p.m. of sulphur dioxide are satisfactory for safety, whereas twice as much is necessary where the acid is deficient.

It is for this reason that citric acid is added to the sterilizing solution given in your wine book. But remember that while the acid addition improves the bactericidal efficiency, the mixture will deteriorate more quickly, so if you keep a stock solution for this purpose it should not be stored for long periods. It is recommended that you omit the acid until you are ready to sterilise your apparatus.

EVER ONWARD
93. How long has the modern winemaking movement been in existence? Can you let me have some milestones in its development?

To answer this in any detail would take too long. Anyhow, here are a few outstanding events.

Andover claims to be the first founded Circle, officially founded in March, 1954, although there had been meetings before that.

The first issue of the *Amateur Winemaker* was in December, 1957, with a circulation of 500. It sold at 6d per copy, with 14 pages, of which 5 were advertisements.

In the same year, Captain Treadwell had organised a Convention of Winemakers at the County Farm Institute, near Winchester, which we are told "gave a tremendous impetus to winemaking in the country".

The Hampshire Rally for Winemakers in 1958 was

numerically a flop, although there were 31 Clubs in existence at the end of this year. The idea of an annual National Convention still raised doubts in some minds: "It might invite unwelcome legislation . . . it might prove expensive to operate.".

Nevertheless 170 people attended the First National Congress at Andover in 1959, and in 1960, at the Second at Bournemouth, there were over 600 show entries. It was clear that it was to be an annual event, so on 29th October of that year 88 Circles were invited to discuss the matter at Andover. Only 20 sent representatives, but a steering committee of six was elected to ensure the continuity of the National Conference and Show, and a voluntary contribution of 1/- per member per Club was invited to cover expenses. All of us there felt the importance of the occasion, and we were convinced that the "Annual" would now live up to its name.

In the same momentous year the Wine Clubs of Hertfordshire came together to form their First Wine Festival, and the editor of *Amateur Winemaker* commented, "The idea of regional organisation looks like catching on, and it is obviously a step in the right direction . . .".

The Annual Conferences grew steadily, and the 2,000 exhibits at Brighton in 1963 showed up the lack of a consistent judging practice. I personally remember one judge whose equipment covered the surface of a medium sized table! A sub-committee examined the problems, and the main result was the formation of the National Guild of Judges, based on the 1964 National judges as founder members. The publication of a Judge's Handbook in October, 1964 set up a code of behaviour, and an examination for future judges was prepared.

Because there was no link between Circles, outside the Regions, Cyril Berry proposed a resolution at the National Conference of 1964 for allowing Circles to have a definite system of affiliation to a National Organisation of Winemakers. It was launched in May, 1965 for both Clubs and winemakers as individual members. It has never been 100% successful, and has been much criticised as not constituting a true national association of clubs.

It is interesting, therfore, to see a movement towards the federating of Federations started last year in 1973, which appears to be moving towards a new National Association by means of a tiered system. We shall wish it well, for unity is strength, and there are ominous signs that we shall need that strength in the days ahead.

COMMERCIAL GIMMICKS

94. *What is your opinion of high-sounding names being given to simple chemicals, which are then sold at inflated prices by commercial firms?*

This is an old grumble, and some people get hot under the collar about it, It is true that often simple and common substances are given important titles, decked out in fancy packs and offered at many times their basic chemical value. For example, potassium carbonate plus a little glycerine may be advertised as an Acid Reducing Agent; ammonium sulphate with Vitamin B or some dried malt becomes an Atomic Enervator; methylated spirits is elevated to a Pectin Detection Solution, and so on.

The fact to realise is that the cost of such goods is the price of ignorance on the part of the purchasers. One can understand beginners availing themselves of these, but there is no reason except laziness for not acquiring a little wine theory as time goes by, and then purchasing the constituent chemicals at a reasonable price from winemaking stockists. There are excellent books on winemaking nowadays, and I have little sympathy with those who cannot be bothered to understand the process of winemaking, and then moan about the price they have to pay for proprietary equivalents.

On the other hand, there is no doubt that firms catering for winemakers' needs provide us with a real service. A wide range of apparatus, small amounts of chemicals, packed ingredients, modern developments, all available under one roof, so that a single journey or a postcard fills up our stocks. There is no compulsion, except clever advertising, to buy gimmicks, and if suckers are taken for a ride they should start a little self-education in the rudiments of their craft and hobby.

HARD WATER

95. *What exactly is meant by hardness in water? I know that the deposit in a kettle is the result of this, but what chemicals are involved in causing this, and how does hardness vary from district to district?*

Hardness in water is related to the content of the salts of magnesium and calcium. There are other salts in solution in most waters, but these two are those most affecting the relative hardness of them. Their content depends on the district where the water is found, so that there is considerable variation over the country.

If these salts are bicarbonates, i.e. magnesium bicarbonate and calcium bicarbonate, then the water containing them is said to be of "temporary hardness", because boiling it drives off carbon dioxide, and insoluble carbonates are precipitated out, clinging to the sides of kettles and pans.

If however they are sulphates, i.e. magnesium sulphate and calcium sulphate, the the water is said to be of "permanent hardness", because boiling has no effect on them, and they still remain in the boiled water.

It is beermakers whose product so largely turns on the use of the right water for the particular brew, the permanently hard water of Burton suiting the pale ales produced there, and the soft water of Dublin benefiting the famous stout. Winemakers seem to be less affected, for we use so much less water, but there is sufficient for some winemakers to claim that wine can be affected in the same way, and to experiment with different waters for different wines.

It might be worth noting also that salts of temporary hardness promote alkalinity, and those of permanent hardness increase acidity.

See also Question 9.

HELPFUL CLUBS

96. *Are Clubs doing all they can to assist and teach beginners? I feel that we beginners tend to be forgotten in the Club I attend; everything is geared to experts.*

I can only answer this from the Clubs that I know or visit during the year, but if these are indicative of the wine movement as a whole, then the answer is Yes, they are assisting beginners.

The proportion of beginners in any Club varies from few, where there is a long waiting list for membership and not many new entrants come in during the year, to those with a large turn-over, which may have as many as 50% beginners. It is difficult to find a lecturer who can suit both beginners and experienced members when he speaks to the Club. Usually he will adjust his talk for one section or the other according to his subject, for often efforts to please both at once only results in something that suits neither.

Consequently, the majority of Clubs ask their new entrants to be tolerant of lectures that are above their heads, and then cater for them specially, such as by running inter-meeting discussions and demonstrations, or by a special course of lectures, or by running a panel of trouble-shooters on call each month, who are prepared to visit winemakers in their homes to assist with problems arising.

These days new winemakers stay beginners for a far shorter period than the old pioneers. So much knowledge and experience is at their disposal in the form of books, evening classes and helpful colleagues, that the fumbling in the dark that some of us remember so well is no longer necessary at all.

So, by and large, there seems little need to be dissatisfied as a beginner in a Wine Club. If you feel you have a real complaint in your own circumstances, then speak to a committee member about it, or bring it up at the A.G.M. Do not harbour a grudge. The Club is for every type of winemaker.

JUDGES QUIZZED
97. To what extent does personal preference enter into wine judging, and must this be accepted as inevitable?

As judges are human and not computers, they have preferences, but as far as possible they endeavour to detach themselves from these, and they succeed to a surprising extent.

For example, we all have one or two favourite types of ingredients, assuming that the wine is not blended, but if these turn up in say a Table Class, it is not so difficult to put aside one's preference so that all are judged impersonally from the point of view of their being suitable for the table. If blackberry is my favourite fruit for wine, it is unlikely to interfere with my noticing a fault in a blackberry entered for the competition, or sensing the superior merit in another fruit entered, although this latter may not be one to which I am particularly partial.

The real difficulty in getting away from personal preference, is when one reaches the final three or four taken from the selected short list. Here, it may well happen, and it often does, that there does not seem to be a whisker of difference in merit between them; all are of excellent quality. It is in such a situation like this, *all other things being equal*, that it becomes extremely difficult, perhaps impossible, not to resort to one's natural preference for that particular flavour and bouquet that has brought most delight in the past to nose and palate.

It is for this reason that some judges feel that out of a class, the top three or four selected should be rated as "Top of the Class", and not graded again into 1st, 2nd and 3rd, an invidious job for a judge when, as *may* happen, the 3rd is as "good" as the 1st. But it seems that this is what entrants want, and it is likely to continue therefore until they show that they want a change.

PROOF SPIRIT

98. What is the origin of the term "proof spirit", and why is it not the same as percentage of alcohol?

The term seems to have originated before hydrometers were used. Spirits were considered to contain about 50% alcohol, and to test this standard, gunpowder was damped with the spirit being tested. If the powder still ignited and burned quietly, then the spirit passed the test, but if not the spirit contained too much water and too little alcohol for the gunpowder to burn, and the spirit was declared as being "under proof".

Later in 1816, Sykes' hydrometer was adopted for official purposes, and a definition offered. This was that proof spirit weighs 12/13ths of an equal volume of distilled water at, presumably, 51°F. The meaning of this is that Proof Spirit contains 57·1% of alcohol by volume at 60°F, the temperature usually quoted.

If we call Proof Spirit 100, then absolute alcohol or 100% alcohol, would be represented by 175°, or, if you like, 75° over Proof.

The important thing is not to regard degrees proof as synonymous with percentage. To change degrees proof into percentage, multiply by 4/7. Thus whisky, which is 70° proof, contains 40% alcohol by volume.

THE FRENCH WAY
99. *I noticed in the wine list of a Wine Shipper that the alcohol content of wines was given in "degrees Gay-Lussac". Is this the same as degrees proof in England?*

No. Gay-Lussac was a French physicist of the 18th century whose hydrometer has a scale indicating the percentage of alcohol by volume. It is normal in France to quote alcohol content with reference to this hydrometer, or merely to indicate the number of degrees without his name. This number is the same as the percentage of the alcohol content.

THE LAST WORD
100. *You may remember that when you were on our Club Quiz Panel you told me that the odd flavour I described in my wine could be a germ or something of that sort. Well, now it turns out that my small son, in a fit of temper because he couldn't go out, had poured some dish water into the must. What do you think of that?*

I give up!

INDEX

The numbers refer to the questions.

Acetaldehyde, 45
Acetic flavour, 67
Acids
    Choice, 27
    Content, 4, 12, 44
    Excess, 34
Air-lock, 6, 52
Alcohol
    Age, 36
    Cereals, 12
    Content, 79, 99
    Evaporation test, 69
    Gravity, 41
    Oxidation, 45
    Potential, 25
Amino acids, 12, 46
Anthocyanins, 32, 33
Ascorbic acid, 42, 63
Autolysis, 12

Benzoic Acid, 42
Bicarbonates, 9
Blends, 33, 34
Bouquet, 38
Bufferage, 4, 20

Calcium, 43
Campden tablets, 81, 92
Cask storage, 36, 65, 89
Cereals, 12, 80
Chlorine, 3
Citric acid, 27, 38, 92
Clearing
    Natural, 47
    Pectin, 50
    Starch, 68
    Tannin, 24
Clinitest, 71, 72, 73
Cloud, 33, 75
Clubs, 96
Colour, 32
Commercial wines, 88

Dessert wines, 78, 85

Fermentation
    Aerobic, 6
    Checking, 16
    Failure, 23
    Spontaneous, 19, 31
    Sticking, 56, 69
    Troublesome, 37, 42
Flower wine, 28
Flowers of wine, 60
Fluoridation, 7
Fortification, 85
Fusel oil, 12, 46, 76

Glucose, 39
Glycerine, 73, 74
Grape juice, 13, 20, 28
Gypsum, 84

Haze, 33, 39
Hydrometer
    Alcohol content, 69
    Alcohol effect, 41
    Dry wines, 71
    Fixed factor, 79
    Potential alcohol, 25
    Sugar content, 72
    Unfermented solutes, 82

INDEX

Hydrogen sulphide, 29

Invert sugar, 1, 2
Isinglass, 57

Lactobacilli
  Encouragement, 61
  Mouse, 48
  Troubles, 21
  Viscosity, 62
Lactose, 53

Maderisation, 59
Malic acid, 27, 38, 61
Maturation
  Bottling, 54
  Cask, 65
  Clouding, 75
  Period, 51, 87
Metabisulphite, 18, 81
Mineral salts, 14
Mould, 10
Mousy wine, 48
Must reduction, 49

Orange wine, 26
Oxidation
  Cask, 65
  Curing, 63, 66
  Pre-fermentative, 44
Oxygen, 6, 52

Paraffin, 15
Pasteurisation, 37
Pectin, 43, 50
Phenol oxidase, 44
Plastic containers, 90

Potato wine, 46
Potassium carbonate, 34
Proof spirit, 98

Racking
  Halting fermentation, 16, 52
  Helping clearing, 47, 50

Rhubarb wine, 30

Saccharin, 58
Saké, 80
Sherry flavour, 45
Sodium hydroxide, 40
Sorbic acid, 16, 42, 86
Stabilisers, 42, 86
Starch
  Haze, 39, 68
  Fermentation, 12, 80
Succinic acid, 38
Sugar
  Cane, beet, 22
  Invert, 1, 2
  Test for, 71, 72
Sulphite
  Anti-oxidant, 44
  Campden tablets, 81
  Clearing, 50
  Excess, 55
  Late addition, 29
  Stabilising, 42
  Stock solution, 18, 92
  Sterilising, 10, 31
  Two kinds, 18
Sweet wines, 16
Syrup clouding, 11

INDEX

Tannin
Clearing, 47, 50
Excess, 57
Test for, 24

Tartaric acid, 27, 38, 84
Titration
    Commercial wines, 4
    Palate, 8
    P.p.t. sulphuric, 77
    Store life, 40

Ullage trouble, 35

Vinegar flavour, 67
Vitamins, 14, 42

Water, 3, 9, 95
Wine judges, 97
Winemaking movement, 93

Yeasts
    Quantity, 5
    Surface, 64
    Wine, 17, 83

Other "AW" Books

PROGRAMME IDEAS
—the AW's printed list to help programme secretaries and others; how to construct a year's Circle programme; where to obtain speakers (on winemaking, brewing, commercial wines and allied subjects) films, coloured slides, social events and ideas, suggestions for outings, wine competitions, list of judges, etc., etc.

MAKING INEXPENSIVE LIQUEURS
—add that touch of luxury to your winemaking with this first class full length paperback dealing with the intricasies of liqueurs, their making and their history.
Ren Bellis

STRAIGHT-FORWARD WINEMAKING
—this book is written for the winemaker who appreciates the non-technical ways of making wine but avioding the legendary folk-lore stigma that has clung to 'Home Winemaking' for so many years. Precise and very readable.
Prof. G. W. A. Fowles

TEACH YOURSELF WINEMAKING
—a concise 262 page handbook that takes the beginner right through the initial trials of winemaking and brewing painlessly, up to expert status.
Duncan Gillespie

WILD PLANTS FOR WINEMAKING
—the Countrymans' or womans' guide to picking programmes throughout the seasons. With easy reference, plants are under the heading of the month they appear either in fruit of flower. Ideal for town-dwelling maker of country wines. 87 pp.
T. Edwin Belt

MAKING CIDER
—the **only** book currently available on this fascinating and ultra-British craft. Recipes for sweet, dry, still and sparkling cider. And cider cookery.
Jo Deal

Send for our Price List

WINEMAKER'S DICTIONARY
—the most comprehensive and readily available mine of information. Most easily consulted reference book for winemakers, lecturers and shop staffs.
Peter McCall

100 WINEMAKING PROBLEMS ANSWERED
—if you have a winemaking problem you are sure to find the answer in this new book by author, wine judge and lecturer, Cedric Austin, who over the years has compiled the most common faults and problems that beset the winemaker and answered them in one handy book.
Cedric Austin

BREW YOUR FAVOURITE PUB BEERS
—do not be restricted to drinking what your local brewery dictates. Now you can, with the help of this book by T. Edwin Belt, brew the beer that was once available over the bar.
T. Edwin Belt

WINES FROM YOUR VINES
—the logical sequence to Mr. Poulter's first book 'Growing Vines'. Readable and very practical, covering all aspects of winemaking from grapes.
Nick Poulter

THE BIG BOOK OF BREWING
—this "fat paperback" is the most advanced textbook for any home brewer covering all aspects of the craft. 256 pp., fully illustrated with photographs and line drawings.
Dave Line

WINEMAKING WITH CONCENTRATES
—for the first time we publish a book entirely devoted to making wine with the various fruit juice and concentrates now available to the home winemaker. Either a British or Canadian edition is available. Please state which you require.
Peter Duncan

Send for our Price List

OFF-DUTY WINEMAKING

—this book has been written to allow the newcomer to winemaking to make his or her first gallon of wine with the minimum of fault and subsequent disappointment. Easy to read, easier-to follow instructions.
90p, postage 18p

FIRST STEPS IN WINEMAKING

The acknowledged introduction to the subject. Unbeatable at the price.

C. J. J. Berry

SCIENTIFIC WINEMAKING—made easy

The most advanced and practical textbook on the subject.

J. R. Mitchell, L.I.R.C., A.I.F.S.T.

THE WINEMAKER'S COOKBOOK

Gives a whole range of exciting dishes using your home-made wine.

Tilly Timbrell and Bryan Acton

WINEMAKING AND BREWING

The theory and practice of winemaking and brewing in detail.

Dr. F. W. Beech and Dr. A. Pollard

GROWING GRAPES IN BRITAIN

Indispensable handbook for winemakers whether they have six vines or six thousand.

Gillian Pearkes

"AMATEUR WINEMAKER" RECIPES

Fascinatingly varied collection of over 200 recipes.

C. J. Berry

WINEMAKING WITH CANNED AND DRIED FRUIT

How to make delightful wines from off the supermarket shelf.

C. J. J. Berry

Send for our Price List

PRESERVING WINEMAKING INGREDIENTS
Includes drying, chunk bottling, deep freezing, chemical preservation etc.
T. Edwin Belt

HOME BREWING SIMPLIFIED
Detailed recipes for bottled and draught beer plus know how.
Dean Jones

RECIPES FOR PRIZEWINNING WINES
Produce superb wines for your own satisfaction!
Bryan Acton

WHYS AN WHEREFORES OF WINEMAKING
Assists the winemaker to *understand* what he is doing.

THE WINEMAKER'S GARDEN
All you need to know about planting the garden for winemaking.
Duncan Gillespie

HOW TO MAKE WINES WITH A SPARKLE
Discover the secrets of producing Champagne-like wine of superb quality.
J. Restall and D. Hebbs

130 NEW WINEMAKING RECIPES
Superb collection of up-to-date recipes.
C. J. J. Berry

MAKING WINES LIKE THOSE YOU BUY
Imitate commercial wines at a fraction of what they would cost to buy.
Bryan Acton and Peter Duncan

THE GOOD WINES OF EUROPE
A simple guide to the names, types and qualities of wine.
Cedric Austin

Send for our Price List

ADVANCED HOME BREWING
The most advanced book on home brewing available in this country.
Ken Shales

PROGRESSIVE WINEMAKING
500 pages, from scientific theory to the prduction of quality wines at home.
Peter Duncan and Bryan Acton

HOME BREWED BEERS AND STOUTS
The first and still recognised as the best book on this fascinating subject.
C. J. J. Berry

WOODWORK FOR WINEMAKERS
Make your own wine press, fermentation cupboard, fruit pulper, bottle racks, etc.
C. J. Dart and D. A. Smith

BREWING BETTER BEERS
Explains many finer points of brewing technique.
Ken Shales

HINTS ON HOME BREWING
Consise and basic down to earth instructions on home brewing.
C. J. J. Berry

MAKING MEAD
The only full-length paperback available on this winemaking speciality.
Bryan Acton and Peter Duncan

Send for out Price List

PLANTS UNSAFE FOR WINEMAKING
—includes native and naturalised plants, shrubs and trees.
T. Edwin Belt

GROWING VINES
Down-to-earth book for the viticulturalist.
N. Poulter

DURDEN PARK BEER CIRCLE BOOK OF RECIPES
How to make a whole range of superb beers.
Wilf Newsom

JUDGING HOME MADE WINES
National Guild of Judges official handbook.

Send for our Price List